The Gap Year Handbook

An essential guide to adventure travel

Tim Beacon

Visit us online at <u>www.authorsonline.co.uk</u>

ISBN 0 7552 0201 5

Authors OnLine Ltd
40 Castle Street
Hertford SG14 1HR
England

Printed in Great Britain

This book is also available in e-book format, details of which are available at www.authorsonline.co.uk

The Author

Born in 1961 Tim Beacon has had a varied life. He has travelled widely and run his own part time adventure training company since 1988. He qualified as an Operating Department Practitioner in 1987 and spent many years working for the NHS in a variety of clinical and teaching roles. He was awarded a Post Graduate Diploma in Travel Medicine from Glasgow University in 1999. He also has a successful background in business and is actively involved in church and charity work, including running an aid organisation that supplies Developing World hospitals with redundant medical equipment. Tim is married to Sarah. They have three daughters and live in Bedford.

Acknowledgements

A book like this requires lots of input from a lot of people. With this book there are two individuals in particular that have made this book possible, namely Sandra Grieve and Dr Hugh Matthews. I first met Sandra when we were both studying for our Post Graduate Diplomas in Travel Medicine at Glasgow University. Her knowledge on the subject is encyclopaedic and her support, encouragement and advice along the way have been invaluable. Hugh and I go back many years. He came on the inaugural Outdoor Experience course when he was 17 years old and still doing his A Levels. He is now a fully-badged GP! Hugh's advice, based on many years' experience in the outdoors, travelling, and as a doctor, has, as always, been brilliant, wise and diplomatic. Sandra and Hugh's enthusiasm and commitment have been a real inspiration along the way. They have read the text many, many times!

Of course, there are many others who have had a major input. Mention must naturally go to my wife, Sarah, who has both supported and tolerated me attempting to type at my laptop at all hours and has also made many of my travelling adventures so much fun.

Then there are all the others who have offered encouragement and contributed to the text. Hugh's wife Karie has been a complete star, going through the text in minute detail and coming up with numerous very sensible suggestions in the process. Bronco Lane, another one of the Outdoor Experience team, has written on jungle survival and generally encouraged me throughout the writing of this book. There are many others who in various and important ways have contributed along the way: Mum and Dad, as always; Steve and Sue Allen; Kit Barger; John Black; Nigel Bradshaw;

Andy Burrows; Alistair and Eve Burt; Barry Cheesman; Elizabeth Fewkes; Bob Handley; Dave "Geordie" Hind; Dave Jordan; Simon Kanjee; Pete Kelly; Terry Sambrooks; Adrian and Jane Shutte; Paul and Jackie Stedman; Derrick Simms; George Storrow; and Keith Willett.

Finally, the contributions of those that have written of their experiences have been much appreciated: Richard Chadwick; Phil Cox; Sarah Hancock; Andy and Sally Snelson; Chris Snelson; Mike Watson; and Ruth Williams

All the above and many others have played a part and have themselves a story to tell. Thanks to them all.

This book is dedicated to:

My wife and children, Sarah, Ruth, Rosie and Harriet.

Mum and Dad, who have always encouraged a spirit of adventure in everything and yet always had wise words of advice along the way.

The Intensive Care Unit at Shrewsbury Hospital NHS Trust. Without their skill, care and dedication in October 1997, my wife would not have a husband and my children a dad.

Paul Millard, 1951-2000. An inspirational instructor who is greatly missed.

All the instructors at The Outdoor Experience who over many years have given me tremendous support, diplomatic and sensible advice and generally made running courses so much fun.

Contents

1. INTRODUCTION   **1**

2. PLANNING YOUR ADVENTURE   **2**
Organised and semi-organised adventures   2
Independent travel   9
Making the choice   11
When and where   11
Parents   12
Finance   12
Tickets   14
Insurance   15
Visas and work permits   17

3. EQUIPMENT   **19**
Footwear   19
Personal clothing   22
Other bits and pieces   28
Carrying your kit   35
Photography   38

4. STAYING HEALTHY   **44**
Getting advice   45
Vaccine-preventable diseases   49
Diseases carried by insects   58
Stomach and bowel problems   68
Water   69
Food   72
Pre-existing medical conditions   77
Deep vein thrombosis   78
Women's health   79
Teeth   83
Eye care   84
Skin care   85
First-aid (travel survival) kits   86

PHOTOGRAPHS 93

5. ON YOUR WAY 97
    The airport 97
    Arrival – culture shock 98
    Accommodation 99
    Food 100
    Transport 101
    Communication 109

6. MONEY AND PERSONAL SAFETY 112
    Safety and security 112
    Money management 113

7. PERSONAL AND CULTURAL ISSUES 115
    Getting on with people 115
    Sex, drugs and rock 'n' roll 116
    Hearts and minds 119

8. MANAGING YOUR TIME – WORK OR PLAY 125
    Choosing your activities 126
    Wild country adventures 130

9. SURVIVING IN ADVERSE ENVIRONMENTS 134
    Emergency survival skills 134
    Mountains 136
    The jungle 143
    Deserts 146

10. WILDERNESS FIRST AID 150
    Minor ailments 151
    More serious medical conditions 153
    Being an expedition medic 172

11. RETURNING HOME 173

APPENDIX: 176
    Websites 176

1

INTRODUCTION

In today's modern world, people of all ages are heading off all over the world, absorbing the multitude of cultures and experiences that are on offer. There has never been a better time to explore the planet and to live life to the full. Travel can develop self-confidence and build a person's life skills, and your adventure will create memories and friends that will last a lifetime.

Whether you're going to work on a project in a remote village in the developing world, or a journey from country to country having a go at every activity available, with sunbathing and the odd bit of casual work thrown in, you will want to get the most out of every second. And that's the purpose of this book – to help you achieve the adventure you want. Like anything in life, travel and adventure can be risky. You can just buy a plane ticket and jet off to a foreign country with no preparation or guidebooks. However, you're more likely to have a good time if you use this book to do a little bit of valuable planning before you go. Time spent on preparation is rarely wasted. By reading this book you can leave on your adventures better prepared, more confident and able to get the most from your experiences.

This book has been written with 'Gap Year' travellers in mind, who have traditionally taken a break from study to spend a year or so exploring the world, and it focuses on people who will be undertaking more adventurous travels rather than seeking work placements in a Western country. Today, though, 'gap years' are no longer confined to students, and whatever your age, whether your adventures are for weeks, months or years, the information that follows will help you to have a more enjoyable time.

Whatever you do, wherever you go, remember one thing: Life is not a dress rehearsal, so plan it, get it right and go for it!

2

PLANNING YOUR ADVENTURE

So you've decided to take time out, but where do you start? Like all good things, the basic principles can be written down on the back of an envelope at the pub. However, behind a successful and worthwhile venture there is more organisation and preparation than you may realise. This particularly applies if you have not been travelling before. Fail to plan, and you plan to fail. This is a big adventure; it's costing a few bob, so make it work.

So what kind of trip are you going to choose? You could go off with organised or semi-organised groups, on your own or with friends. All have pros and cons; it's simply a case of thinking it through and doing what's right for you. It is also possible, and often quite easy, to combine one of the organised options with some independent travel.

ORGANISED AND SEMI- ORGANISED ADVENTURES

If you want to go on an organised or semi-organised trip, the options are:

- Gap Year companies and charitable organisations
- Expedition companies
- Summer camps in the USA
- Adventure tour operators

Sometimes the distinctions between these can be a bit blurred. The most important factors in making these trips a great experience are a sense of humour, a positive frame of mind and good preparation.

Gap year companies and charitable organisations

These organisations put you (normally with one or more companions) into isolated environments, usually in the developing world, to carry out some form of long-term purposeful project or role such as teaching. Generally most run for about three months, although it is possible to take part in quite long projects, some lasting eight months or longer. If the project is properly managed by the sending organisation and the participants are trained and supported appropriately, these can be mind-blowing experiences. Initially, you may find it a considerable challenge, with a steep learning curve, but the depth and quality of the experience can be really awesome.

While on these longer trips, you may be able to arrange your own mini-excursion, and the sending organisations often build time into the programme for this. Many people also undertake some independent travel at the end of the organised project.

All charities and companies involved with this type of trip should have signed up to a code of conduct and include proper training and debriefing as part of their service. For detailed current codes of practice check out the web page of the Year Out Group, http://www.yearoutgroup.org/index.html.

Recently, some charities have set up projects where they take you to a developing world environment for three to four weeks, to soak up the culture and see at first hand what the charity is doing. If this sort of work interests you and ties in with what you want to achieve, it may be a good way to get a taste of what you might experience before committing to a longer project. While you are not committed to a lengthy stay if it's not right for you, the negative side is that you may just be getting into your trip and have settled down in the new environment when it is time to come home.

There are a wide variety of organisations running projects abroad. The size of the sending organisation and the price of the trip can vary significantly. It is important that you know what they expect from you, and who you are responsible to while you are working in a foreign country. You need to be clear how you are going to be supported and you need to check very carefully what they are actually offering, as there is a lot of variation. Pay attention to areas such as accommodation and how much preparation they give you, both practically and in the form of written information.

Ruth, whom I originally met when she was doing her (first!) gap year in Uganda, recently sent me an e-mail updating me on her adventures on her second gap year in Zambia. Somehow, in between she is fitting in a degree.

I've been in Zambia for just over four months and it's been a really interesting time so far, an eye opener in many regards. Like most African countries it is a land of contrasts; contrasts between the rich and poor, the literate and illiterate, the wet north and the drier south, the traditional way of life and the emerging Western way of life and values, and between belief in spirits and demons or God. Last term I took an evening course learning about marriage and family life in Zambia, which gave me an insight into why things are done in traditional society and the meanings behind different events.

I have been helping at a community school in town for street children, playing games with the children and helping them in a drama competition and attempting a few basic English lessons. The first lesson that I taught them was learning the parts of the body in English. After drawing a picture of the body on the blackboard we tried to label the parts. I found it very challenging trying to teach the children when some could not read the word 'arm' or 'head', I didn't know where to start! The children are really good fun and I love watching them dancing and singing, they are so uninhibited and have amazing harmony and sense of rhythm. We have been going out to a compound called George Compound to teach a group of ladies how to sell the knitted goods that they have been making. Another English lady taught 50 or more ladies how to knit and make baby clothes and the ladies wanted to sell these items but didn't know where to start. We taught them how to work as a team, how to handle money, keep records, cost the goods, quality control, guard their capital, etc. After a few weeks many groups diversified into selling vegetables, paraffin or fish and had built up their capital to be able to sell larger goods. At the end of January we are visiting them again to see how their businesses are going and to provide support for them. I learnt that one of the ladies had lost her only two children through diarrhoea: she had been unable to treat them and they had died. At the moment I am in the process of compiling a Bemba translation of a leaflet that I have written on diarrhoea, explaining how you get it, how to avoid it, how to make an oral rehydration drink and how to eat a balanced diet. After finishing the diarrhoea leaflet I'm hoping to write leaflets on burns, fever, controlling bleeding, sprains, etc, and then translate them all into Bemba. We had a fantastic time in Livingstone, white water rafting down the Zambezi, seeing the Victoria Falls and flying over them in a 1930s Tiger Moth, which was incredible! We hopped across into Botswana to go to Chobe National Park and see all the elephants. There are over 70,000 elephants in the park as well as many other game; a feast for the eyes! Sunset cruise on the Chobe river, watching hippos in the water and crocs sunbathing on the banks and an amazing sunset. It was good!

Expedition companies

These trips tend to range in length from one to three months, and typically combine a mixture of aid work (such as a building project or teaching local children), exploration (for example going on safari, climbing a mountain or rafting a river) and relaxation, perhaps finishing on a beach. They often consist of large groups and they can be quite expensive and involve a lot of fundraising. You don't have to worry about the organisation and you are guaranteed an adventure, with a lot of the risk managed for you. From the feedback I have had, participants find them positive and highly enjoyable. A potential drawback is that you can't choose your companions, although generally they tend to be like-minded. You are also ultimately in the hands of your leaders on the ground, so you have less control over what you do and when you do it; you can't have a day off because you don't feel like trekking or working that day! You should also remember that you will need to do some thinking for yourself, be organised, be able to get on with people and be a team player.

Phil had a great time on his three month expedition, as he describes:

> *Quite simply the time of my life: I went to Zimbabwe, for an expedition of three months. I built elephant pens, learnt how to track rhino, did wildlife and tree surveys for the World Wildlife Fund which involved trekking for six days in the middle of nowhere, white water rafted the Zambezi from the Victoria Falls for five days, ate wild food, built a clinic and taught in a local school.*
>
> *It was well run, and had the ethos of letting us learn from our mistakes. It taught us to think for ourselves, and about who we were, and gave us the opportunity to lead our group. It also showed us how we reacted to dangerous situations (including poachers, rhinos charging, running*

out of water in the bush, poisonous animals and people being cut with machetes). If you think this is fun, then don't miss the opportunity of a lifetime!

Richard went on a shorter trip and also had a great time:

"Challenge" is the word. Students have ownership of their expedition from the planning phase right through to its execution. It can be quite costly, but when travelling to remoter, wilder, more exciting parts of the developing world, it's important to have total confidence in the support systems should anything go wrong. I have experienced this at first hand – and it works! Working on projects with wonderful people from poorer parts of the globe can be the most rewarding of experiences.

Summer camps in the USA

A popular summer job is to work on young people's camps in America, which are very much part of the American way of life. There are several organisations that deal with this. I worked for four summers on these camps and a terrific experience it was too. Depending on how you do it, they may simply provide a visa and work permit and leave the rest to you, or they may organise the lot. I turned down the first camp I was offered, after doing some research and realising that this camp would not have been the best for me. As a result I was placed in a superb camp, and spent the summer running backpacking, rock climbing, rafting and canoeing trips along the East Coast of America and up into Canada.

You may be going with an organisation, but you will still have to think. The adventure training programme at the camp I went to had become almost non-existent, and I had to start from scratch in a new country with a week to get a programme sorted. It presented a considerable challenge at the time; however, it worked, was developed and was still being used years later. The whole experience was so positive that I made my own arrangements to return the following summer. The youngsters can be very spoilt at some camps, but you can soon bring them round. Americans are very friendly and this is a great way to spend a summer in the USA and get paid too. Like many of these organised adventures, it can be done on its own or incorporated into longer travels.

Adventure tour operators

These companies advertise in adventure travel magazines and newspapers. The trips may be as short as two weeks in Morocco or as long as six months driving across Africa in a truck. You can also use a short trip as part of a longer period of travel. By their nature, they generally involve smaller groups than the expedition companies discussed earlier, and everyone has to do their fair share of the work. You can't choose your companions and the longer trips will throw significant challenges and adventures at you on a daily basis. They can, however, take an enormous amount of organisational hassle out of your trip and often visit more unusual places which might be difficult to travel to on your own.

I went on a ten-day trip with a local operator to Lake Turkana while in Kenya, and had a great time. Hugh Matthews, The Outdoor Experience medical officer, went on a six month trans-Africa journey. Here are his thoughts:

> *After leaving school I booked to go on a six-month journey from England through to South Africa, in a converted truck. I hadn't met any of my fellow travellers before I turned up at the port, and as with all groups of people thrown together it took a while to get to know each other. The leader was very experienced, which was invaluable, and knew a lot of the best places to go to, but being in a big group does reduce your flexibility and ability to make your own plans. It also means you spend less time talking to local people. However, having the truck meant we could go*

places that would be very difficult otherwise and the experience as a whole was very positive. It showed me countries and cultures I had never thought about before, and gave me confidence to travel on my own at the end of the trip and during the following year.

INDEPENDENT TRAVEL

Whether travelling with friends or by yourself, it means more preparation and planning compared with the organised trips, although both styles have their own unique challenges. The main advantage of independent travel is autonomy – you choose when and where you go, how long you spend at each place, and who you go with. You may also meet a wider range of people on your travels than on an organised expedition, both locals and other travellers. These advantages can be significant. An additional benefit to going as a pair or as part of a small group is that it may be cheaper, as you can share certain expenses.

So does this style of travelling present any problems? You may decide you don't want to be with your companions and have differing ideas of what you want to do, or if you are on your own you may feel lonely. If this all sounds a bit depressing, remember that you can have these issues at home. It is just that when travelling you need to be more flexible, reasonable and understanding, as it isn't always easy to separate, so it's best to try to resolve any minor disagreement over plans. You will also have to do more planning and research than if you were going on an organised trip – though for many independent travellers this is part of the fun.

A lot of the potential problems of going as a pair or small group can be sorted out at the planning stage. Do you really have a similar mindset and do you want the same things from the trip? Do you have similar attitudes to money and the activities you want to do? If one person does not like spending money and wants to live on the cheap while the other person likes to spend a bit more freely, you may have a source of conflict. Thinking about these basics is common sense and can save you a lot of trouble later on.

It definitely pays to have an objective, especially at the beginning of the trip. Longer-term plans inevitably change and this is to be expected, but at the beginning of your adventure having something to go for and get stuck into gets you into the swing of things rapidly and focuses the mind. You don't necessarily have to commit yourself by booking things in advance. Pre-booking the first part of your trip can give considerable peace of mind but, for example, trekking agencies can often be sourced on arrival at your destination. Nepal is a great example. We sorted out a short trek around the Kathmandu valley the day after we arrived, and left the next day.

Independent travelling is likely to leave you with memories that will always make you smile. I remember Sarah and I arriving tired and hungry, in the early hours of the morning, at a strange town in Northern India. It was pouring with monsoon rain and it had been a long and tough journey, during which we hadn't been particularly convinced the bus was even going to where it was supposed to! Eventually we found a hotel; it's all part of the experience. Travelling with a small group of friends is great but it can be challenging, and you will need that all-important sense of humour. You'll certainly learn about your companions and their flexibility and capability during your adventures. It is important to be sensitive to your companions and support each other – we all have bad days.

If you go solo there can be a tendency to worry about being lonely. Clearly there will be times when this is true, but you will normally find the opposite is the case as you mix with a wide variety of people on your travels. I remember going off on my own around Europe when I was nineteen. Backpacking around the Tour Du Mont Blanc long distance path, I met some great people; 48 hours after my departure I was laughing and joking with some of them in a high mountain refuge, having had a terrific meal with a glass of wine while a thunderstorm raged outside.

MAKING THE CHOICE

How do you choose what to do and which company to go with? Personal recommendation can be a useful guide. Talk to people who have travelled independently and those who have travelled on any of the types of organised trip that you are interested in. Check out the itinerary and talk to the companies where appropriate. Look at what the information is like and the cost, remembering you don't get something for nothing. Periodically there are adventure travel exhibitions, which are worth a visit as you can look at a lot of different trips to see which one might interest you. Once you've done some of these things you should start to develop a feel for which part of the world, style of adventure and company is right for you. Develop this instinct and listen to it; it can help in all sorts of situations.

WHEN AND WHERE?

When deciding where to go, there are a staggering number of resources available to find out useful and current information. Key sources are the Lonely Planet and Rough Guide series of books. These give detailed information, including history, politics, climate, accommodation, approximate living costs, transportation, available activities and the best times to do them, and so on. Other sources are the internet, people who have been travelling there themselves, and tourist offices for the country. When choosing your destination, safety could be an issue. Undoubtedly, some areas are more dangerous than others and whilst you do have to keep things in perspective, this is a factor in considering where to go. You should listen to Foreign Office announcements and visit their website.

You are going to have to do your research to work out the best times to be in the areas you wish to visit. You may, for example, wish to go trekking in the Himalayas. If the only time you can travel is at the height of the monsoon it would be fairly pointless, as you won't see much and will get very wet. If you can wait or you can afford to bring the trip forward, your Himalayan trekking plans are a more realistic option, otherwise you should plan a trek elsewhere.

PARENTS

As parents can get worried and stressed by the notion of an adventure, it's a good idea to consider them when you're planning your trip. Yes, the risks to life and limb do exist everywhere, even when nipping to the local shop, but getting your mum to trust your judgement may require considerable persuasion. Having your parents buy into your ideas is a good move and they may even have suggestions that are worth listening to, honest!

FINANCE

The first thing to say about money for your trip is – you need to have some! It is likely that you will have to work, and believe it or not (and you probably don't!), this is part of the experience. Going to work is a necessity in life, but don't despair – you may be surprised who you meet when you are working, particularly when you tell them what you are saving for. A lot of people have travelled, or want to, so you could find a like-minded soul, which would help to keep the dream of your adventure alive.

If your employer knows you are saving for a Gap Year adventure, they'll realise that they will get some hours out of you and that you are unlikely to go off sick. When you go to get a job, remember to look smart and to have an attentive, interested and professional attitude. You need that job; that mountain, beach, safari, bungee jump and so on is waiting! The idea of the forthcoming adventures should make you moderate your daily spending at home, as you focus on all the amazing things you might want to spend this money on during your travels.

If you are going to work on an organised project, you may well find that there is money available from charitable sources. Your library should have a directory of grant-making trusts, either in book form or on CD-ROM, whom you can contact. Before you write off to everyone on the list, make sure you fulfil the rules of the grant-making body you are applying to, as the administrators of the trust or charity cannot consider applications that do not meet their criteria, regardless of their merits. There is also a time issue, as many grant making bodies only meet to give out funds a few times a year. Be professional and honest in your letter and accompanying information. Tell them about yourself, what you are going to do and what you hope to achieve, and personalise your application using the information that you are given in the directory for each charity you write to. With modern word-processing packages there is no excuse for a badly presented application, and it's always useful to double-check it by getting someone else to read it through. On return, you should give the people who have funded you some form of report detailing what you have done and how it has benefited you and others. It's also a nice idea to send them a postcard or two whilst you're away. This is polite and gives a good impression, which will help others who apply for funding for similar projects in the future.

Many factors are likely to influence your travel plans and your money requirements. You may decide to work in your home country to fund your adventure abroad, saving enough to cover all the expenses (along with a credit card back-up), or you may want to accumulate the bulk of your likely expenditure but hope to supplement it by working abroad. Whichever way you decide is best for you, how far your money will stretch depends on which country you're visiting, how you intend to live and the activities you are hoping to do. Sleeping and travelling by the cheapest means possible, doing lots of hiking and exploring with economical safaris will obviously make your money last longer than if you live in expensive accommodation and intend to learn to scuba dive, fly or bungee jump. It is important, however, for you to realise that even if you have opted for more basic standards of living, you are extremely likely to encounter activities and places you didn't plan (or budget) for. It's best to have a top-up fund for such unknowns, as most people do return from their adventures owing money.

You will need to work out some sort of budget – but a word of warning: Don't get obsessed with trying to live too cheaply, as it can be a false economy. The dingiest place in town might be cheap but you might get food poisoning, your kit is more likely to be at risk of being stolen and, of course, walking around these areas at night is more risky. I remember when we were in Kashmir staying on Dal Lake in the fantastic houseboats. We paid about £1 a day extra and got a really nice boat with a terrific view. Others tried to save money by living a little cheaper. Their boat was not nearly so nice, the view was not so good and one person got food poisoning, ending up on a drip. This curtailed their plans to explore somewhat and was a lousy way to start their trip. You may only visit the places you are travelling to once in your life, so do not spoil it when a small amount of money will make a big difference.

TICKETS

If you are a bargain hunter then this is an area for you. There are many options, from the internet, through student-orientated ticket shops, to travel agents. It can be complicated, but a good switched-on travel agent can be a valuable asset, and often no more expensive than spending hours on the internet. Going locally can mean it's easier for you to sort out any problems, and it means you can forge a relationship with the company. On occasions I have struggled to find sensible prices and information from the internet and traditional student companies, so I have gone to a local travel agent instead and I've usually got the ideal flight at a better price in ten minutes. Whoever you book with, make sure you use an ABTA or ATOL bonded organisation as these offer protection in the case of the airline or travel agent going bust (and this has happened to several well-known airlines in the last few years). Paying with a credit card can offer some measure of protection.

Tell the travel agent where you want to go and when, and see what they come up with. You need to be careful of penalty clauses if you change dates or times for your flights; some flexibility on the dates of your return flights can be very useful. Get several quotes and do check carefully, as there often seems to be little logic to variations in airfares from the traveller's point of view. Prices can vary significantly just because you are, say, flying at a weekend or the wind is coming from the west when there is a full moon! My mum was once offered £250 by a major airline at Heathrow if she took a flight 5 hours later. She had only paid £260 for the flight in the first place.

Don't forget that a good travel agent can sort out ferries, coaches, rail tickets and the like. It can be cheaper to get these in advance, but this is not always the case – you'll need to check. You may not want to book too much before you leave as it will reduce your flexibility to change your plans. Do some research to make sure you get what you really want for the right price.

Finally, once you buy your ticket and have parted with hard-earned cash, buy your travel insurance without delay in case something happens and your trip has to be cancelled for genuine reasons.

INSURANCE

Do not skip this bit. A decent insurance policy is absolutely vital. Like travel vaccinations, if you can't afford it, don't go. Too many people leave these shores with inadequate insurance – don't be one of them; buy a comprehensive policy, not a cheap one with inferior cover. Fortunately, there are many companies which now provide insurance for adventurous travel: it's quite a competitive market, so prices are fairly reasonable. Use any recommendations from friends, check out adverts in adventure travel magazines and see what your travel agent has to offer. Then look at the policies in detail and see which is the most competitive, taking into account the extent of the cover. Bear in mind the cheapest are not normally the best. Remember that you will need emergency dental cover as well as medical cover, as this sometimes varies.

Most policies aimed at backpackers and adventurous travellers are very realistic and will allow you to do a number of adventure sports on an occasional basis. However, it is important to be honest, as they have extra premiums for longer term or higher risk activities. If you intend, for instance, to do rock climbing, mountaineering or deep sea SCUBA diving, you may have to take out an additional specialist policy for this period, as your normal backpacker policy will not cover it. If in doubt, check. It is very important that you get this right, even if it costs more.

In the unlikely event that something happens, whether it is theft, illness or a major problem at home, you will be very glad you had it sorted. Remember that the USA and Canada are much more expensive in terms of healthcare, so if you are spending time in these countries, the premium may be increased. You also need to check to see what valuables are covered and the limits for each item.

On a thought-provoking note, an incident happened once when I was leading a canoe trip in Canada. A gentleman in the group sadly died suddenly in the back of his Canadian canoe, from a previously undiagnosed heart problem. The insurers were superb and were straight on the case; however, the undertaker in the local town seemed reluctant to do anything. He explained that he had seen many such policies in his career and over 50% had not paid up, so until he got a fax from the insurance company he refused to do anything. This duly arrived within the hour and the body of the deceased was back in the UK within 48 hours, as was his wife and a friend of hers.

One major consideration with your travel insurers is how they deal with emergencies. For major situations such as a significant accident, a stay in hospital or even repatriation, they will organise everything for you and arrange payment. For more minor situations such as emergency dental work or small scale theft or damage, you may need to pay and then claim it back – it depends on the company. Check the small print so you know what your immediate liabilities will be.

To give you an example of how differently the insurance companies work, I once checked out the issue of pregnancy and travel insurance as a result of a question asked at a Travel Health seminar I was running for GPs and nurses. Two reputable companies gave vastly differing answers. One would not insure pregnant women as they say it is two people and there are all the issues of special care if a baby is born very prematurely. The other considered it a natural state and did not alter their premium until after thirty weeks of pregnancy. Okay, the vast majority of people reading this book won't be pregnant when they travel, but it makes the point – so check policies carefully.

VISAS AND WORK PERMITS

These can be a lot of hassle as, apart from anything else, the entry regulations for developing-world countries in particular seem to change with monotonous regularity. This is an area where guidebook advice and even the internet may be wrong, so contact the relevant embassies direct to find out. Also, remember that there is a distinct difference between visitors' visas and working visas, in that the former are usually easier and cheaper to get, but will not allow you to seek employment during your travels. Work permits can be complex, and can depend on what you plan to do, whether it is paid or voluntary and the length of time involved. It is sensible to check these issues well in advance of departure. If you are going as part of an organisation they should, of course, have this covered; but do check, as penalties for breaking the rules can be severe.

You may have to visit embassies or post your passport. If posting, send everything recorded delivery as it's not something you can afford to lose. Make sure that your passport is not going to expire imminently as this will cause unnecessary problems. Most countries need your passport to be valid for six months after your intended date of return, so if yours isn't, get a new one before applying for any visas.

Finally, some countries may require Yellow Fever vaccination as a condition of entry. While there are few other immigration medical requirements, there are usually a lot of other diseases that you need to think about getting protected against, and this is covered later in chapter four, Staying Healthy.

3

EQUIPMENT

You could survive comfortably on your travels with next to nothing, living out of a tiny rucksack and using your initiative. Alternatively, you can have an enormous rucksack with every gadget known to mankind in it, and in reality not use most of them. As always, there is a sensible middle ground. If backpacking round the world, you are generally going to be carrying everything you need with you, for a significant time. It makes sense therefore that your rucksack is not too heavy or cumbersome but yet the kit in it allows you to survive comfortably in any situation – any fool can be uncomfortable. On the other hand, if you are going to be staying in one area for a long period of time, packing can be simpler and you may be able to take more clothing and other items with you, as you will not have to carry them everywhere. Don't forget, though, that you might change your plans or travel elsewhere after you leave your fixed base.

Before deciding on the kit you need and what to pack, you need to think about where you are going, what you are going to do and when you are going to do it. For example, if you need trekking kit for the first part of your trip, you could post home the items you don't need once you are in a suitable country and have finished with them. If you are then proceeding to hot climates you can buy clothes as you go, and your clothing will be lighter anyway. You can have equipment posted to you, particularly if you are doing a project with a fixed base, though postal and customs delays make this a less reliable option.

FOOTWEAR

You are likely to spend a lot of time walking around, and it is absolutely vital that your feet are comfortable and preferably dry. For general travelling a good stout pair of trainers is ideal and there has been an explosion recently in the number of trainers suitable for adventure travel. Footwear is one area where I find that you get what you pay for, so do not skimp, and make sure you buy them well in advance of your trip in order to make sure they are broken in and comfortable. All-nylon uppers tend to leak like a sieve and I don't think they are as comfortable on your feet as leather. Uppers that combine leather and nylon can provide a good balance. Your footwear needs a good gripping sole with a bit of rigidity and laces that aren't too long and won't come undone.

It's a good idea to look in the adventure travel magazines and go to a good outdoor shop to see what's available. Take advice from the shop assistant. Everyone's travels are different, and a good assistant will take time to understand your needs and be interested in what you are doing, so that you get the footwear which is right for you. If they aren't, go elsewhere.

If your trip is going to involve trekking you may already be sorted with regard to walking boots. If not, the same rules apply. However, with boots it is even more important that you make sure they are comfortable and right for you before leaving. You get what you pay for, and you don't want your trek to be ruined by blistered, sore and wet feet.

Once, just before leaving on an expedition to Kenya, I bought a new pair of boots and did not allow time to break them in or check they were right for me. We climbed Mount Kenya's walking summit, 16,000 feet high (and, incidentally, a fantastic trek!). Unfortunately, coming down the mountain I was in agony as my toes were rammed into the front of the boot. I left the boots back in Nairobi and collected them when we finished all our other exploring. I sold them as soon as I got home.

Assistants in a good quality outdoor shop will be able to give you advice. Boots are there to give you good foot and ankle support, keep your feet dry (unless you are deep in water), and not to give you blisters. Some people trek in trainers; possibly you can get away with this, but I would always go for a pair of boots. Lighter weight boots are available, some using Gore-Tex for waterproofing, and while I personally don't find them as comfortable as leather, you might feel they are right for the trip you're planning.

If you plan to go trekking, you can face a bit of a dilemma, as you will probably need boots for trekking and trainers or other lightweight footwear at other times, but will not want to carry spare footwear around with you. While on the trek, you can often leave your trainers back at the central starting point, but what happens when you don't need your boots any more? They can be a bit of a nuisance to carry in your rucksack and too cumbersome to wear all the time, so if you don't need them, post them home. Do check the reliability of the postal system, as some countries have a tendency to 'lose' packages. Ask around, and check in your guidebooks.

Now you have gone out and bought some decent footwear, what next? Well, the posh footwear is not going to be very effective unless you have some good socks and these can be expensive. If you are backpacking and regularly on the move it pays to have a couple of pairs of really good socks; believe me, it is worth it in terms of comfort. If hiking, your best bet is to get some good loop-stitch walking socks to go with your good boots. You must have at least two pairs, one of which must stay dry, but three pairs are better. If your boots do get wet you'll have to put wet socks on as otherwise you will just make a dry pair wet; quality socks make this a more comfortable process and you are less likely to get blisters. Putting wet socks on in the morning is not pleasant but they soon warm up. Avoiding this unpleasant start to the day is preferable.

It often pays to have both long and short socks. During the day short socks will do, even if it's fairly cold, but there's nothing like a nice long warm pair of socks in the evening. A few pairs of bargain socks can be useful - the sort you can bin and replace as you go – but as noted above, a couple of pairs of quality lightweight socks are a worthwhile investment. How to avoid insect bites is covered in more detail later, but long socks that don't leave your ankles exposed when you sit down in the evening will reduce mosquito bites.

The other footwear you may want to consider is a pair of lightweight but sturdy beach sandals. They are great for casual use, for the beach, or if you are going rafting. There are several things to consider, though. They don't protect your feet from thorns or bites, they don't give any real support and they are not warm (which is pretty obvious). Sandals can be made from leather or rubber. Rubber dries much quicker, which is a considerable advantage as this type of shoe often gets wet, but leather ones are more comfortable and less sweaty. You can buy cheap sandals once on the road and bin them before you move on, if they are worn out or you cannot fit them into your rucksack.

PERSONAL CLOTHING

It is a hard fact to accept, but you cannot take an infinite supply of clothes with you; unless you are my wife, in which case you will try! You are going to have to be selective in what you take. You need hard-wearing, practical, quick drying, lightweight and low bulk items. This means, for instance, that jeans are often not suitable.

There are many makes of travelling trousers in the shops these days, made up of various materials. They roll up to a small volume, dry quickly and are very lightweight. Some makes are extremely expensive whilst others are very cheap, and to be honest I have not noticed much difference between cheap and expensive ones. I wore a pair of cheap poly/cotton trousers pretty much every day for a year and, whilst they were somewhat battered at the end, they were still good enough to cut the legs off and use as shorts for a while longer. There is a trend for trousers with zip-off legs, but I'm not a fan of these. They seem a bit uncomfortable and, more importantly, what if the zip breaks whilst you are in an isolated and cold environment?

Most trousers will have multiple pockets, which is useful, although sometimes finding your wallet can be hard as you always try the wrong pocket! Having said that, multiple zipped pockets, some being hidden, can help to make your wallet more secure. Make sure they have a good belt, as you don't want it to break as you travel, and that they will tighten up if you lose a few inches, as travellers often lose weight.

Many backpackers will travel in hot climates for some of the time, so shorts are necessary. There are lots of different makes available with varying price tags, and the same principles apply as for selecting trousers (again it is worth having some good pockets).

My wife tells me that any lightweight skirt will do, although you can get travelling skirts, which have good pockets and are made of quick-drying material. Skirts can keep you cool but do remember that in certain cultures women will be expected to cover their legs. Women wearing shorts or miniskirts may cause offence or even be breaking the law; check these things before you go. Skirts and crop trousers aren't so good at stopping insect bites in the evening, so you will probably want to take some long trousers for evening use.

To complete the bottom half you will need some underwear which is comfortable, practical and washes easily. What you find comfortable at home in hot weather is likely to be suitable although activity underwear for men and women is available in some outdoor shops, designed to wick away moisture when trekking. If you are heading into colder climates, you can also buy warm, lightweight thermal underwear.

On the top half, in hot climates you will often be wearing T-shirts, which can usually be bought as you go. Long-sleeved shirts are also useful as they provide greater sun protection, are warmer in the cool evenings and give some protection from insect bites (and therefore associated diseases such as malaria). If the temperature drops, the key to staying warm is the layering principle – several thin layers will keep you warmer than one thick layer. A fleece top to keep you warm during cold days and chilly nights is a really good move; even deserts can be cold at night. Fleeces make nice pillows too, particularly on long bus journeys. They can be a bit bulky but their versatility and comfort outweigh this. Fleeces come in varying weights, and I would recommend one that is not too light, preferably with a zip for control of ventilation. Take advice, research your trip and consider whether you are the sort of person who feels the cold or not. Clearly, if you are going into the high mountains you are going to need more than a single fleece top. For extra warmth there are some excellent lightweight down jackets and vests available, but remember that down is hopeless if wet.

You will normally have to carry your clothing as you travel, so you have to be discerning as to how much you take. It's a balancing act – often you won't use a lot of what you take but when you do need it, you'll be glad to have it! Use common sense and research local conditions before you go.

Waterproof clothing. Clothing works best when it is dry. As you wander the world it will almost certainly rain, sleet or even snow on you at some point. If you are in hot, tropical conditions, then you are normally better off just getting wet when it rains and changing in the evening, before you go to bed. However, if you are in more temperate conditions with wind and rain, you will need to keep yourself dry to stay warm. You may not plan to go into these conditions but plans can change and you don't always know where you will end up. For instance, Africa has some high and exciting mountain ranges that can get cold and wet.

Getting wet is miserable, uncomfortable and at its worst can lead to hypothermia which can be life threatening. Getting wet as you travel is also rather pointless as there is a very simple solution – carry a set of waterproofs. A lot of travellers carry some sort of rain jacket, few carry waterproof overtrousers. You could find yourself in a situation where you have to walk a couple of miles to a hostel in a downpour. You would, I suspect, be very glad that you had a good set of waterproofs with you so that you could arrive at the hostel nice and dry. Knowing that you can stay dry at any time is a comforting thought. It comes back to the basic survival principle of shelter – that's what waterproofs are: a simple, portable shelter which will keep off the wind and rain.

I recommend taking a waterproof jacket of reasonable quality, and would also advise you to think about whether a pair of lightweight waterproof overtrousers might come in useful on your travels. So what waterproofs do you take? How do you choose? How much do you spend? Go into any outdoor shop and the walls will be lined with jackets of every conceivable size, fabric, colour and quality. In a good shop you should get appropriate, commonsense advice, suited to your travel plans. A bit of research does not do any harm and allows you to have an informed discussion. The big stores and manufacturers have excellent catalogues and there are also a lot of smaller shops around with a great range and excellent, enthusiastic service.

There are many different breathable materials available these days with different advocates and prices. I have used Gore Tex a lot but have also used jackets with various other types of breathable material, which have lasted and functioned equally well. Good quality shops, with good brand names, do not generally sell rubbish as it would not help their long-term business prospects. You don't need jackets that you would use on the top of Everest, so buy the jacket which is appropriate for your needs. If you are on a tight budget, you can't afford a breathable jacket and you don't think you'll need one much, there is an easy alternative – buy a non-breathable waterproof jacket. These are commonly used by outdoor centres and for the Duke of Edinburgh award, and are approximately a quarter to a third of the price of a posh breathable jacket. The disadvantage is that you can sweat in them, although I used one for years and never found this a major problem. If you arrive slightly damp on a high Himalayan pass in a snowstorm, as my wife and I have done, so what? Given how damp we would have been without them, it did not seem that important! They tend to be longer than the more expensive breathable jackets and are therefore not so fashionable.

A suitable jacket should have the following features:

- Good-quality hood attached to the jacket. A peak to it and a face guard are good as they really keep the elements off. Remember how much heat is lost through the head.
- Pockets are very useful but you don't need too many as they just add to the expense. A couple of good hand-warmer pockets, preferably zipped, and a chest map pocket under the storm flap are adequate.
- Zips. These must be covered by a good storm flap or they will leak.
- Good cuffs are important as water getting up your sleeves is uncomfortable. Velcro ones are very good.
- Draw cords at the bottom keep out draughts and are a must in really bad weather. Waist draw cords can help and add a touch of style.

Overtrousers will generally be used a lot less than a jacket, if at all. Personally, I still take them wherever I go. I think lightweight breathable fabrics with long zips are best, so that they are quick and easy to put on and take off. Overtrousers get a bad press for being uncomfortable and sweaty, but in wet muddy conditions, for example trekking, they can be a real asset. With modern breathable fabrics, sweat is not the problem it was, and they keep your clothes and legs dry, clean and warm. Think about your own travel plans, and consider whether it might be useful to pack a pair – and, as with boots, if you do not need them later on you could send them home.

Other bits and pieces of personal clothing you may need are:

Hats and gloves. What you take will depend on what your plans are. Your research should give you some idea of the weather and what you will need. If trekking or going to potentially cold areas, a hat will do an enormous amount to keep you warm and comfortable and should be regarded as essential. Estimates vary but between 30% and 60% of body heat is lost through the head. There are all sorts of fleece hats around at various prices. Some have a breathable outer covering and a peak. If you are heading into wilderness or colder environments these are terrific.

Bush hats are also important. They offer protection against the sun and have an important role in the prevention of heat illness. They can also keep the rain or snow off your head and can be pulled over your eyes when taking a nap. I find the cloth bush hats best as they crumple up nicely into a pocket and dry quickly. White ones reflect light but can be a bit loud. In hot climates I have soaked such a hat in water and it has really helped to cool me down.

There are all sorts of gloves and mittens available should you need them. Mittens are warmer than gloves, so you may prefer them. You can get nice fleece gloves and mittens some of which have a breathable nylon outer. Surprisingly these are not as expensive as you may think.

Swimming costumes. Be sensitive and show respect to your host country as getting on with local people and behaving in a responsible manner will maximise your enjoyment abroad. Therefore women should consider local customs; for instance in some countries it may be inappropriate to wear a bikini. For men, swimming trunks that are like shorts are best as they can be used as normal shorts as well.

OTHER BITS AND PIECES

There are lots of things to consider here, in no particular order of importance:

Sleeping bags. Do you take one? This can be a tough call. They can be bulky and may be rarely used, depending on your plans. On the other hand, when they are needed they really *are* needed and it's great to have a nice warm night. I prefer a good night's sleep, preferably in the dry, and taking along my sleeping bag pretty much guarantees this. Again, it depends on your objectives. Generally, I know that when travelling I will be doing some trekking and exploring in the back country, which means I am likely to need one.

Sleeping bags are often divided into categories of warmth, such as two season, three season, and so on. This is a bit nebulous although it does give you some idea of the warmth of the bag. Other factors will affect your warmth and the sleeping bag's effectiveness. These are: what you have eaten (and hence how much heat you are generating), the amount of insulation underneath you, where you are, the humidity in the air and whether or not the bag has a hood.

There are two types of sleeping bag fillings to consider: namely, natural fillings (down) and synthetic. The advantage of down is that it is lighter than synthetic fillings and much less bulky when compressed, for a comparable amount of warmth. Synthetic bags are cheaper than down (often by a lot), still keep a certain degree of warmth when wet and are much quicker to dry if they do get wet. They are bulkier and heavier, though compression straps can help keep the size down.

Features to look out for include:

- Zips down the side, which should have a baffle behind them to prevent heat loss

- A hood – remember, the head loses a lot of heat
- A shoulder baffle to keep in warmth around the shoulders
- The construction, particularly for synthetic bags, as the warmth can be affected by the way they are made.

You do need to take advice and choose what's best for you. I think if you are going to take a sleeping bag then one with a hood, shoulder baffle and zip are essential. You can then pull it right up around you in the cold, open it up and use it as a duvet or lie on top of it if it's warm. If it's really cold you can put on clothes inside your bag to stay extra warm so you don't necessarily have to take a bag suitable for the worst case scenario – just make sure your clothes are dry (see my note in the rucksack section)!

I recently came across a kind of travelling blanket that had buttons on it to make a basic poncho or sleeping bag. It was very lightweight and compact and it seemed a good compromise if you weren't at all convinced you needed a proper sleeping bag. A silk sleeping bag liner is also a really useful bit of kit, particularly in hot weather. It will protect you from bugs in unknown beds and is comfortable, light and compact.

Sleeping mats. These are for lying on when camping or sleeping out under the stars. They are essential if you are doing this as you lose loads of heat through the ground and they also give you something softer to lie on. If you know you are going to be sleeping in tents or mountain lodges and you are either on your own or you don't think the trekking agency you are going with can supply them, it's a good move to take one as they are so important in making you comfortable. You can buy them in Nepal quite easily but less so in places like the Indian Himalayas and Africa. Do some research before you go to establish whether you need one. They are bulky and are a pain to carry around if you are not going to use them. Most people roll their mat up and strap it on to their rucksack. If you don't want to cart it around after you have finished trekking or camping, give it away. We'll look at their other uses in the emergency aid section.

Thermarests are an alternative sleeping mat, and are more comfortable than traditional insulating mats, though I don't think they are as practical or hard wearing. If you are camping for weeks or months they may be preferable.

Nylon tarps. These are sheets of nylon with holes around the edge for tying cord to. You may want to consider one of these if you are thinking of adventuring a bit. I have seen these advertised recently as 'jungle bashas' and you can get them in army surplus stores. They have a lot of uses, apart from sleeping under. They are good for sitting on, creating shade, putting over dodgy mattresses that may have half the cast of 'Bugs Life' in them, or making a shelter during a storm. I have even used one as a sail on a canoeing trip in Canada, when the wind was behind us.

Breathable sleeping bag covers ('bivi bags'). These are generally made of Gore-Tex and can be quite expensive, although I have seen some bargains in army surplus stores. Unless you're into serious trekking or sleeping out, they are not worth taking, but if you end up in a leaky tent supplied by the local populace then a protecting bag around your sleeping bag will be worth its weight in gold. You can also sleep under the stars and not worry so much about a bit of rain or heavy dew. Some have mosquito netting in the entrance, which is very useful. I trekked with friends around parts of New Zealand, including the Abel Tasman Park, up into the mountains and along the coast. We had a lot of fun and slept out under the stars without any problems, using nylon tarps, sleeping mats and bivi bags.

We will look at mosquito nets in chapter four, Staying Healthy.

Penknife. This is an essential for camping and is useful for many types of travel. Personally, I am a complete Swiss Army knife fan

– expensive for a penknife but worth every penny. Buy one with a red handle so you can find it when you've dropped it. 'Leatherman' gadgets are becoming popular now, although they are more expensive than Swiss Army knives. Make sure they have scissors on them. This is an ideal gadget for Great Aunt Agatha to buy you before you go walkabout, but do not pack it in your hand baggage when travelling by air, or you will very rapidly be minus a penknife.

Torch. Electricity can go off at night, especially in the developing world – that's if there is electricity. There are lots of different torches available, from posh head torches to a basic small single AA battery torch. One point to make your life easier: don't buy some incredibly cheap and nasty torch from your local DIY shop. It will break and fail. Buy something that is of a reputable make such as the small Maglites, which are popular, reliable and hard wearing. A bigger torch will be too heavy. There is a variety of excellent head torches available and some are very lightweight. Good makes of torches have spare bulbs in them but if they don't, put a spare bulb (along with batteries) into your first aid kit.

Gaiters. If trekking, particularly in temperate climates, these can be useful in keeping your feet, socks and trousers clean and dry. There is some crossover between these and overtrousers but they undoubtedly have a place, particularly if snow is involved. If you are not trekking they will not be necessary. You can always post them home when you have finished with them.

First-aid kits. We will be discussing the contents of your first aid kit later in chapter four, Staying Healthy. I like to think of these as a travel survival kit. In other words, apart from holding plasters, bandages, headache tablets, sterile needles and so on, it can contain lots of other bits and pieces. These can include spare batteries and bulbs for your torch, a plug for sinks, nylon cord (which has a multitude of uses, all of which we'll cover later), a candle for power cuts, matches, spare malaria tablets and spare contact lenses, to name just a few items.

Washkit. This is straightforward and obviously there is a lot of personal preference here. It can include soap, toothbrush, toothpaste, comb, shaving stuff, contact lens bits (if you wear them), tampons, etc, as appropriate. Remember, you will have to carry everything, so consider buying bits and pieces while you are travelling. Essentially, you don't need much if you think about it. A towel is necessary – one smaller towel is usually sufficient as your large, favourite towel that you use at home will be too bulky.

Clothes washing. When I was first travelling, I waited for a sunny day and stood in the shower with my clothes on, in an attempt to clean them. Then I took them off, put clean clothes on and dried the wet ones. It seemed reasonable to me, although my mum was less sure! This was not a very effective way of cleaning my clothes (although it was easy). What I did subsequently (at my mum's request) was to take a small bottle of washing detergent for use in a sink or bath, or if one was available I used a laundrette.

In many areas of the developing world, local people will wash your clothes for you at a very reasonable price. This is convenient and socially aware – it gives the local people a bit of money. I remember giving our clothes to a gentleman in India late one night. He wandered off with them and returned with them beautifully pressed and cleaned the next night, and he'd even replaced missing buttons.

Sunglasses. These are essential. Sunglasses are obviously necessary in bright sunlight, but if you are travelling in the back of an open taxi, pick-up or safari truck, they can keep the dust out of your eyes. You can buy them cheaply abroad but, wherever you get them, make sure they offer protection against ultraviolet light. In the UK it is often possible to obtain these from good quality chemists or garages. It is, of course, possible to buy designer glasses or ones from outdoor shops which are outrageously expensive for no more protection. Remember, though, that if you are going to extremely high altitudes or trekking on snow, you need eyewear designed for these environments to avoid snow blindness. See chapter four, Staying Healthy, for more on eye protection.

Water bottle. This is a seemingly insignificant bit of kit, but can be life saving. It makes sense to carry some water with you, particularly on a long bus or coach journey as dehydration is horrible and pointless. A one litre capacity water bottle is therefore a good idea. Quality metal ones are best, as they are less likely to leak when being thrown around in your bag. If you buy water, you can pour it into your good quality bottle, as you don't want water leaking onto your paperwork, camera and so on.

Office. Travelling inevitably means a certain amount of paperwork needs to be carried, such as passport, tickets, travellers' cheques, money, letters and notepad. There is a large variety of nylon organisers available which are great for storing this kind of admin material. Do remember that it can pay to keep some of your paperwork apart; for instance, money, which should ideally be stored in several places. We look at personal security later in chapter six, Money and Personal Safety.

Maps / compass. You won't need a compass unless you plan some serious back country travel, but you should take maps of where you are going. One of the best places to get maps is Stanfords in central London. They do mail order and are incredibly helpful. They sometimes have maps you can't get in the country you are going to, although usually you can buy the maps you need when you are there. Your research should tell you the state of play in this area.

Mugs and eating utensils. You don't normally need a full cutlery set or a plate, but a good sized plastic mug and a spoon is a good idea.

Toilet paper. Apart from its obvious use, it can also be used instead of tissues. Always have a roll with you and keep it in a sturdy polythene bag, as the paper attracts the damp.

Short-wave radio. If you are going to be isolated and away from Western media, a short-wave radio can be a Godsend. It can keep you in touch with what is going on or simply be something to listen to when you are chilling out. It can be fun to see what radio stations you can pick up in the middle of nowhere. The posh radios have clocks and so on built in.

Discman. Some sort of Discman for listening to CDs, or an MP3 player, is a commonly carried bit of kit. If taking CDs, get a player with an anti-shock mechanism.

Tents and other specialist kit. Generally you should not need to take a tent or stove, but there may be circumstances where either of these may be a good idea. For example, when we went trekking in the Indian Himalayas we knew from research that the quality of local tentage was not the best and that we could be exposed to bad weather in the hills. We took our own quality mountain tent that we used both in the hills and when exploring isolated rivers by boat. Our assessment of the local tentage and the weather proved correct and to say we were grateful for our tent would be a significant understatement. In Nepal, we did not take a tent as our research suggested the tents would be of better quality. Again, this turned out to be correct.

We have used a military solid-fuel stove on occasions and have enjoyed a brew in some unusual places – both in shabby hotels, where we stuck the stove in a sink, and out on the hills. Remember, it is illegal to carry flammable materials on aircraft.

CARRYING YOUR KIT

Unless you intend to travel mega-lightweight you will need two bags – one small and one large. The small one is for keeping with you on aircraft, buses, trains and so on, as hand baggage. It can hold important documents, money, valuables such as cameras and maybe a bit of spare clothing. It's actually a good move to have enough with you in the small bag to survive on, in case your main luggage goes walkabout in transit. If you are on regular medication this should be carried with you, together with any documentation required for Customs at your destination, such as a confirmatory letter from your GP.

The big bag has everything else in it. But what sort of bag are you going to carry? Travellers are called backpackers for the reason that they tend to carry their worldly belongings on their back in some form of rucksack. One thing is for sure – it can take a real battering as it gets hauled on to every different sort of transport imaginable, falls into streams when the mule carrying it stumbles, and endures tropical rainstorms that you wouldn't believe possible. Your rucksack becomes your friend as you get used to where everything is and it keeps your kit dry with the aid of a waterproof rucksack liner.

So what sort do you buy? What features should you look for? Again a quality outdoor shop that has a variety of makes for you to try on, and that offers good advice, is the best way of finding out what's right for you. All the outdoor magazines have adverts for the different manufacturers and the shops which stock them. It's worth checking out any equipment your friends have, too.

Rucksacks come in many shapes, sizes and designs. Some have multiple compartments in the main body and loads of pockets in just about every place imaginable. Other designs are basically a bag with an internal frame, good straps and a small pocket on the lid. It's personal preference really, although I think simplicity is best. I'm not keen on the rucksacks that convert to holdalls for airline baggage, as I am not sure what they achieve, although I know people who have found them very good.

Internal frame packs are best – in fact, you are unlikely to find external frame models available these days unless you go to America. The internal frames vary depending on the manufacturer, but they are generally comfortable and hard-wearing. They all have well-padded shoulder straps and hip belts, and it is amazing how effective these are in enabling you to carry significant weights comfortably. Try on a variety of rucksacks with weight inside them, as some seem to fit better than others, depending on your body shape.

Your personal needs and the size of your budget will dictate your choice of rucksack. If you are taking a sleeping bag, for instance, the rucksack will need to be wide enough to fit it in sideways. Side pockets are good for having somewhere to put bits and pieces, but make sure you don't put your valuables in them as they are vulnerable to thieves. Some people find the pockets get in the way, but I have not found this to be a problem. Pockets on the lid are useful, but don't overfill them.

Other features which need to be considered are:

- The quality of the material.
- Straps on the outside to hold things like sleeping mats, which can otherwise be hard to pack.
- Elasticated lids to keep out the rain and dirt.
- Extensions at the top which increase the capacity and help to create a weatherproof seal.
- The capacity and shape of the rucksack. Climbing rucksacks tend to be quite narrow.

Deciding what capacity rucksack you need is an interesting issue – 65 litres, possibly extending to 75 litres, is ideal in my opinion. In truth, whatever you have you will fill, and it does depend on what you are carrying. It is possible to get away with a smaller capacity rucksack, but it does not give you much leeway. You may also find that rucksacks of similar capacity can look very different, depending on how the capacity is split between compartments, so use your judgement.

The smaller bag that you use as hand luggage and for general use in town should be fairly malleable and not too big, so that it fits into overhead luggage compartments. Like your main bag it will take a pasting, so buy a good one with a couple of pockets. Some bags fit onto the main pack, which is useful when hiking with both, but I just carry mine separately. If it's in my hands it's harder for people to grab, and I can keep an eye on it and access my camera if I want it.

Waterproof liners. No rucksack is waterproof. They can be pretty good at keeping out the rain, but water has an irritating habit of getting everywhere, so it's best to assume that some water will get in. Having your clothes, sleeping bag or whatever getting wet is uncomfortable at best, but at worst it could lead to hypothermia. Wet kit means a bad night's sleep, which may affect your concentration and lead you to make unnecessary mistakes.

The solution is simple – use a waterproof rucksack liner. These are generally made from nylon. Being a belt and braces person, I line my liner with a heavyweight polythene rubble bag, which can be obtained from a builders' merchant. Bin liners rip, so don't use them.

Put everything you want to keep dry (including your sleeping bag and clothing) inside the liner and fold it down over the items to protect them. This way, if anything leaks elsewhere in your rucksack this stuff will stay dry.

I used to run fun survival trips when I worked on the summer camps in America. We would swim across a lake with our kit in our rucksacks, waterproofed as described above. Despite the rucksacks being waterlogged at the end (but still floating nicely) our personal items would be bone dry. Okay, you may not intend to swim across lakes with your rucksack (generally to be avoided, I agree) but what if your rucksack is sitting on the top of a bus, taxi or truck in a tropical rainstorm, or you are walking to your hotel in the early monsoon? You'll be glad that you paid out a few quid for a liner. Sitting in the hotel or backpackers' lodge that evening, having a brew or drinking a beer as you unpack your dry kit, the phrase 'any fool can be uncomfortable' may come to mind.

PHOTOGRAPHY

You are going to visit many great places, see awesome sights and meet some terrific people. It stands to reason that you are going to want to photograph these and look at the results for many years to come. The other great thing about photography is that if you are walking up a hill, taking a picture gives you a chance to stop and rest!

If this is a subject that you are interested in you will have your equipment sorted, but you may be thinking, I can't take all that photographic kit – what do I leave behind? If you're not into photography, where do you start?

I've been fascinated by photography for years and get a real buzz from looking at photos of my trips, especially if they are taken in demanding conditions. I love boring people with my slide shows, though on one occasion I even fell asleep whilst giving a family slide show! To look back at photos from past adventures is great and a sure way of capturing the memories, so it's worth making a bit of an effort.

Firstly, of course, you'll need a camera. There are three types of camera available which are:

- Compact
- Single lens reflex (SLR)
- Digital

These need to be used with the relevant type of film – slides, prints or in the case of the digital camera, memory cards.

Like much of your equipment your camera will take a lot of hard wear, being used most days, on beaches, up hills and mountains, in jungles, on boats, in deserts and so on. You may be in environments where film and batteries are unavailable or of very dubious quality, so a bit of pre-planning is in order.

The pros and cons of each type of camera are as follows:

Compacts. Lightweight and, as their name suggests, compact. These will fit into your pocket and are normally quick and easy to use. This is particularly useful where looking like a rich Westerner is inappropriate, and you don't want to draw attention to yourself. If the camera is inconspicuous it is less likely to be stolen. The good ones take high quality photos and can integrate flash photography in a sophisticated manner, such as fill-in flash if you are photographing someone outside in the shade. The fact that the lens does not detach means that you are less likely to get sand or dirt inside the camera. You can buy compact cameras that are splashproof, which are good for the beach or wet conditions. Some have a zoom lens. This is an impressive list of advantages and it's certainly hassle-free photography.

The major disadvantage is that some have slow lenses, particularly if they have a zoom lens. This means they don't let in so much light, so you either have to use a faster film, which is more sensitive to low light, or use a flash. Faster films can be a bit grainy but the technology has vastly improved, and it's only a problem on very large enlargements. You can't change lenses either, so if you want to do that, you'll need an SLR.

SLRs. If you are into photography you probably have one of these already and know what equipment you want. There are several things to consider. Most modern autofocus SLRs seem to survive well in rugged environments, but electricity does not get on well with water, so keep your camera protected from the damp, and dry it carefully if it gets wet. When it comes to choosing lenses, everyone interested in photography has their own preferences. I use a 24 mm wide angle which has great depth of field and enables me to get a full sharp foreground whilst showing the setting. It's also a fairly fast lens, which is good for low light. I also use a short zoom of 35-70mm and a 70-210mm zoom. I used to use old auto/manual Nikon SLRs but now use a more modern Nikon F601. With its built-in flash and various exposure modes, I must say it is brilliant and has proved very reliable.

Digital cameras. This development in photography has changed things a lot. Digital cameras definitely have their place, with the ability electronically to edit pictures and delete bad ones. I would not take one as my sole camera under any circumstances, so if your main camera is digital, take a compact camera and film as back-up. Electronic data has a habit of getting corrupted, there is a danger that memory cards may get lost as they are so small and nowadays most take rechargeable batteries so unless you are near a power source to recharge the battery, the camera will only work for a limited amount of time.

Buying a camera. Pound signs may well be flashing in front of you or your parents' eyes at this stage. As you wander around the shops you will see a bewildering variety of cameras at a bewildering variety of prices, most of them high! There is a way round this – buy second-hand. Virtually all my cameras and lenses are second-hand, and after many years they continue to do a great job. In this techno-mad world so many new cameras come out each year that there is a thriving second hand market where you can pick up superb cameras at excellent prices. Older models that are no longer fashionable but are quality bits of equipment can be obtained cheaply and easily. What would buy you an average new camera could buy you a superb second-hand one. Whether buying new or second-hand, go to a specialist photographic shop with a range of equipment and staff who take time to understand your needs.

To buy second hand the following rules apply:

- Decide what type of camera you want. If you want good shots with the minimum of fuss then a quality compact camera is best.
- Go to a good photographic shop that has a wide range of second-hand equipment. They should give a guarantee on what they sell, normally three months.
- A leading brand name is preferable.
- Chat to a friend who knows a bit about photography. Take them along when you go to buy your camera.
- Once bought, put a roll of film through the camera. Take pictures using all of its settings, including the flash, to check it is functioning properly. This also helps you to learn how to use the camera. If there are any problems the shop can change it or refund your money.

Carrying your camera. You do need to protect this expensive and important piece of equipment. Compact and digital cameras often come with nylon cases but I would advise buying a more robust one to protect from rain, sand and dust. A darker colour case is less obvious, making it less likely to be a target for thieves.

There are plenty of SLR cases available that also protect these electronic cameras from the elements. They are a good investment, but can make your camera extremely bulky, especially if you have a zoom lens. On occasions, I have put my SLR in my rucksack with a T-shirt wrapped around it for protection, but I would not recommend this – some sort of case is better.

Film. You'll need lots of it, much more than you think. But do you take slides, prints or digital? As I have already said, I think you should have prints or slides as a backup if you use digital. If you intend to give a slide show, to friends and family or to sponsors, you will clearly need to take slide film with you. If not, it will be print film you go for. If you want both, you will need to take two cameras. Compact cameras are extremely light, so this won't be a problem.

Film comes in different speeds, commonly 100, 200 and 400ASA ratings. 400ASA is more sensitive to low light but the photos will be a bit more grainy. 200ASA covers most eventualities and takes into account the slower zoom lenses on a lot of cameras, so will probably be your best choice. Carrying an extra roll or two of 400ASA is a good idea for darker conditions, such as jungles where the light can be quite dull. This applies to slides or prints. If you disagree, then you know enough to make up your own mind. Buy films from a good manufacturer and make sure they are well in date. It's not the time to buy bargain special film from your local supermarket. If you do need advice, go to a proper photographic shop to make sure you get the correct film. You're going to a lot of effort to get away on your adventures, so make sure your photos do your trip justice.

Batteries. Modern cameras generally require substantial batteries to power them, so take spares – it's as simple as that. I was using a digital camera in Africa and when the batteries ran out (fairly quickly) I found that the locally purchased batteries did not power the camera, even though the voltage measured the same as those bought in the UK; so you are better off bringing batteries from home. Murphy's law dictates that they will always run out when you least expect it and need your camera most, just as that classic photo opportunity appears. I remember my batteries failing on the Pacific Crest Trail in Washington State in the USA. Fortunately, because my camera functioned without batteries, my friend could give me the camera settings and I got the shot of a terrific mountain view.

Taking pictures. If you are interested in getting a better than average picture, get a book from your library on how to improve your photos. There are a few available on travel photography and lots of magazines, including one that concentrates on nature photography. A good photographic book can also advise you on how to use your camera in unusual climatic conditions. When I was hitch-hiking in Yellowstone National Park, I picked up a useful tip from a very pleasant National Geographic photographer who gave me a lift. He said the majority of scenic views that are used in the magazine are taken in the first or last hour of daylight. If you look around at that time you will see why, as the light is much better. If you are staying in an area for a while, look at the views you want to photograph at different times of day. You will be able to choose the best viewpoints and light, and the process of observing is a good opportunity to sit down, chill out and have a drink, all in the name of art!

Developing your pictures. Do not compromise on this. The normal routine is that you return from your trip broke and have photos developed in a cheap place or in a smaller size than you would wish, particularly because you have got loads of films to develop. This is not a good idea. In photography bigger is better, so don't have postage stamp size prints done. Go to somewhere that will do a good job, will not use old chemicals and will put the negatives into sleeves. Some will even put them onto a CD for you which will enable you to edit and present your images on the TV or through a data projector (you can have slides put onto CD as well). You will not regret the small extra cost involved in getting the developing done properly. Personally, I use a well known high street store for all my developing. I am very reluctant to post films.

4

STAYING HEALTHY

First of all, please keep all the following in perspective. The information in this section, taken out of context, could stop you getting out of bed. There is a risk of getting the conditions I am going to mention, but the good news is that using your intelligence, together with modern medicine, you can go a long way towards staying fit and healthy, and avoiding compromise to your adventures. You should also remember that this is a brief description of some of the common conditions you might encounter, and is no substitute for taking good medical advice when appropriate.

Malaria, "Delhi belly", typhoid, HIV, hepatitis, rabies, yellow fever, meningitis and tetanus are just a few of the nasty diseases that people think about when they head off on their exotic travels. There are plenty of less common ones, too. To complicate matters further, diseases are contracted through different means. Some are blood-borne, others are carried by insects (our ever-friendly mosquito being a major culprit), by animals, by air and by humans.

As part of your preparation for the trip it is sensible to get in shape, physically and mentally. This does not mean going for marathon runs, but running or walking several miles a few times a week is good, as is cycling or swimming. Getting into the habit of walking or cycling to the shops, instead of using the car or bus will also help. You'll be surprised how much good it does you, in terms of boosting your self confidence, giving you some time for reflection and helping you to focus your mind.

When chatting to people going off on their trips, the conversation normally centres on the following two areas:

• What vaccinations do I need?

- How do I avoid malaria?

  Both are good questions; however, there is more to consider as staying healthy involves a broad spectrum of issues, including the following questions:

- How do I get current and up-to-date travel health advice?
- What vaccinations do I need and why?
- How do I avoid malaria and other insect-borne diseases?
- How can I minimise the risk of Delhi belly?
- How can my common sense prevent me from becoming unwell?
- How can I avoid danger areas attributable to behaviour, such as drugs, sexual health and alcohol?
- Are my teeth healthy?
- Have I got a suitable first-aid kit and do I know how to use it?
- Can I handle an emergency?
- If I am going to high altitude, do I have a basic understanding of high-altitude sickness?
- Do I have good insurance?
- What if I am taking medication or have a pre-existing medical condition?

In this chapter, we will discuss all the practical measures relating to the prevention of disease, such as safe food and water, hygiene and insect bite prevention. Vaccinations are only one part of the disease prevention process. This is a lot to get through, but it's actually interesting and certainly relevant.

GETTING ADVICE

'A wise person learns from experience. A very wise person learns from other people's experience.' An excellent saying, and very true.

Having established where and when you want to travel, a great deal of travel health information is available on the internet and from books. At the end of this book there is a list of websites that have up-to-date information on all the countries of the world. This information comprises details of prevalent diseases, local disease hotspots and how to avoid them, recommended and required vaccinations, and political and personal safety issues. In terms of books, the Rough Guide and Lonely Planet series have travel health sections in their guides. This research process focuses your mind on the whole health issue, and it is an important part of your planning. There are many good travel health books available, if you want to research the subject in more depth.

Armed with this information you need to book an appointment with your local practice nurse. With the surge in all sorts of travel, particularly Gap Year adventures, you should find your local practice is up-to-date on your requirements. This makes for an informed discussion between you both. Alternatively, you may wish to go to a travel clinic, particularly if you are living away from home. A travel clinic specialises, as the name suggests, in travel and so you should be guaranteed up-to-date, relevant and practical advice, although they will charge for this service. They can carry out vaccinations as appropriate, so make sure you have details of your current immunisation status from your home practice.

Highly experienced travel health nurse, Sandra Grieve, has this to say about seeking travel health advice:

> *Seeking health advice is often the forgotten part of pre-travel planning. I will try to impress upon you the reasons for, and importance of, seeking advice well in advance of your departure date. In travel medicine circles we use the term "last minute travellers". You may think that this refers to people booking last-minute bargain package holidays, but in reality it refers mainly to Gap Year or adventure travellers who have had their rucksacks packed for months in anticipation of their trip, but have done nothing about health advice. The main purpose of travel medicine is to*

maintain the good health and safety of travellers abroad, so it is important to identify travel-related health risks in the prevention of disease and illness. Most of you reading this are "healthy" and you should stay that way, but you are responsible for your own health, so do take it seriously. Many studies show that travellers' behaviour changes when they are overseas. Illness, injury or hospitalisation abroad can be avoided if you seek advice in good time, do your homework and heed the advice that you have been given and have read. There are public health implications for the host country, your home country and for the wider community. Speed of travel today means that diseases can be incubating while you travel. Host countries do not want your chickenpox and the home practice does not want to treat your malaria. Individual needs are important, especially if planning a long stay abroad. Knowledge of health status (including allergies), reasons for travel, length of stay, accommodation (rural/urban), transport and proposed activities are vitally important in evaluating potential risks. There are lots of issues to discuss and explore during a pre-travel health assessment; doing it properly will take time. You can help by sourcing information as outlined above; especially important if planning to visit multiple destinations – different countries have different environments and different health regulations. You need to know what the risks are in association with proposed activities and what diseases are prevalent in the countries, especially malaria – if you don't know what it is, how are you going to prevent it? Remember that not all diseases are vaccine preventable – there is no magic potion, the responsibility lies with you! Vaccination sometimes involves courses, spaced by weeks or months to give effective immunity. If yellow fever vaccination and certificate is a requirement for your destination, these must be obtained at least ten days before departure to be legal, if not, you may be denied entry or actually be quarantined. Sanitation (or lack of it), hygiene, and insect-borne disease are more challenging in tropical climates; clothing and accidents may be more important in others. If you have a pre-existing medical condition like asthma or diabetes, a medical check-up will be a wise precaution. Specialist appointments can take time to arrange, so don't leave it until the last minute. It is important to make sure that routine medications are assessed for the destination and that you have enough supplies to cover your trip. Health services overseas may not be up to UK standards and communication may be impossible in remote locations, so give yourself time and sort it out before you go.

VACCINATIONS

Get vaccinated! As vaccinations are often what people first think about when they prepare to go travelling, we will look at these first. Of the diseases mentioned, some are related to food and water, while others are caused by insect, animal or human contact. Blood-borne diseases are also a risk in many countries. Within reason, if in doubt have the vaccination. Depending on where you go, some of the injections may be expensive, but when you are bitten by a dog in an isolated village in the middle of nowhere, you will wish you had paid for the rabies jab. The diseases discussed throughout this book exist. They are real. This was brought home to me on a recent trip to a mission hospital, where I saw many patients with severe cases of malaria, TB, HIV and typhoid. When considering whether to have a vaccine, bear in mind that people staying for longer periods of time and staying in lower standards of accommodation are at higher risk than short-stay holidaymakers – many gap year travellers will fall into the higher risk category.

To risk potentially life-threatening illness when there is a solution is not very bright, and will ruin your trip as well as that of any travelling companions. Your family is likely to end up fairly stressed, too! You need to visit your surgery or travel clinic at least 6-8 weeks before departure, although if time is restricted, still attend.

VACCINE-PREVENTABLE DISEASES

Below are a few of the more common vaccines available to travellers, but there may be others to consider, depending on where you are going and what activities you will be involved with. You must take specialist advice well in advance of departure. It will become obvious to you that many diseases have similar symptoms, but some may settle by themselves, while others need treatment. For instance, a stomach upset can give you all the symptoms of typhoid. It can also mimic malaria and other conditions. So how do you tell the difference? How do you know when to rush to medical aid and when not to? This is a very hard question to answer, but if you feel worse than is normal for a stomach upset or other illness, then seek advice. If you are travelling with friends, look out for each other and ask for their advice. If you are unwell, you should not be preparing food for anyone else.

Hepatitis A. Hepatitis A is a viral liver disease which is spread by the faecal-oral route (i.e. people not washing their hands after they have been to the toilet) and through contaminated food and water; so good personal hygiene is crucial for prevention. If you become infected, you will be infectious before any symptoms appear, until several days after jaundice develops. (Jaundice is a yellowing of the skin and whites of the eyes). The onset is often abrupt, and other symptoms include loss of appetite, malaise, nausea, weight loss, aches and pains, and abdominal discomfort.

Hepatitis A has no treatment, but anyone who develops jaundice should seek medical attention to exclude other causes. You need to rest, and maintain a high fluid intake. Avoid fatty foods and alcohol, as these require the liver to work harder. It will take about fourteen days to recover, although you may feel washed out for a while after, as tiredness and lethargy are the main reminders of the infection. Symptoms tend to be more severe and prolonged in older adults. Don't handle or prepare food for others (not that you are likely to feel like it), or share anything else, like drinks or cutlery.

The vaccine: Hepatitis A is the most common vaccine-preventable infection of travellers. A single injection, with a booster 6 months later, provides immunity in excess of ten years.

Typhoid. This is a bacterial illness which occurs throughout the developing world. The bacteria live in the intestines. To get it you have to swallow infected food or water, which is why personal hygiene is important. In other words, the disease can be transmitted by food handled by the contaminated, unwashed hands of an infected person. The risk is a bit lower in tourist and business centres, where the standards of accommodation, sanitation and food hygiene may be slightly higher. It can be a very serious condition, with all systems of the body being affected. The risk is particularly high in the Indian sub-continent.

If you contract typhoid, it can take from one to three weeks for symptoms to appear. In severe cases there is a gradual onset of fever, headache, loss of appetite, inability to sleep and a general unwell "flu-like" feeling, which gets worse over a two-week period. Without treatment this will get worse. Constipation is more common than diarrhoea in adults and older children. These symptoms could apply to many milder illnesses, so treat the symptoms (using paracetamol, ibuprofen or similar pain relief) and ensure re-hydration is adequate. If your symptoms last more than three to four days and you are worried about typhoid, you will need to get medical help. Blood tests and faecal cultures will be taken, and antibiotics will be prescribed.

The vaccine: The typhoid vaccine is 70-80% effective, so there is still an element of risk. It can be given as a one-off injection, which produces protection seven days after vaccination and gives immunity for up to three years. Alternatively, it is given by mouth as capsules, with three doses each being given two days apart. You are protected seven days after the third dose, and protection lasts for a year. A combined typhoid / hepatitis A vaccine is available.

Tetanus. This bacterial disease, also known as lockjaw, is found throughout the world and can enter the body through any open wound – a pinprick is big enough. Tetanus spores are present in the soil, so the disease cannot be eradicated. It affects the nervous system and can kill through paralysis. Remember, any open wound should be cleaned thoroughly to prevent infection. It is a potentially fatal condition so make sure you have been vaccinated. Signs of tetanus will appear between five and twenty days after injury. The symptoms are irritability, headache, fever, restlessness and spasms of the jaw muscles, which spread to the face and then to the rest of the body, ultimately causing breathing difficulties. Convulsions can also occur. Treatment of tetanus involves advanced hospital care as soon as possible, but while it is very serious it is totally preventable.

The vaccine: In the UK, most people should have had a full course of five vaccinations when they were babies and children, with the last one normally given at age 15. Check your tetanus status with your GP prior to your trip. It may be worth getting a booster if it is more than 10 years since your last vaccination, but if you do get a large wound which is contaminated with soil or manure, you should seek medical help even if your vaccination is up to date.

Polio. The polio virus is close to being eliminated in many Western countries and much of the developing world, but is still endemic in some parts of Asia and Africa. The virus lives in the gut and goes into the nervous system. It is spread by the faecal-oral route (i.e. people not washing their hands) and by coughing or sneezing. Over 95% of people infected with polio will be unaware they have it. In the 5% who feel unwell, fever, headache, vomiting and nausea occur within a 7-21 day period and may lead to neck stiffness and paralysis. Paralysis occurs in about 0.1% of victims. There is no treatment, except rest. If diagnosed with polio, it is likely that you would be admitted to hospital due to the possibility of severe illness.

The vaccine: For many years, the polio vaccine in the UK was given by mouth, although since 2004 it has been given in combination with tetanus and low dose diphtheria. Until the disease has been eradicated worldwide, the risk of acquiring it remains, and all travellers should be vaccinated. As with tetanus, it is given as part of routine vaccination in the UK, but you should have a booster if you have not been vaccinated in the last ten to fifteen years.

Meningitis. This is a high-profile disease due to the mass vaccination campaigns that now take place in schools and universities, for the bacterial 'C' strain. I contracted the serious 'C' strain whilst running a team-building course in Wales in 1997. I survived to tell the tale due to a quick-thinking GP receptionist, a switched-on GP, an excellent paramedic crew and the superb Shrewsbury NHS Trust ITU. None of these exist in the developing world, but the good news is that there is a vaccine for all but the 'B' strain. Transmission is mainly through person-to-person contact; if you are going to be living or working with the local population in an endemic area, be aware and be protected. If you develop meningitis, the lining of your brain and spinal cord swells up and death results from the massive rise in pressure on the brain. You are unlikely to get it, but the best way to protect yourself is to make sure you are immunised. There are five strains, but no vaccine for the 'B' strain, so you should remain aware of the symptoms.

Having had meningitis myself, the symptoms have a familiar ring. They include headache (which becomes extremely severe), loss of appetite, irritability, vomiting, fever, inability to tolerate bright lights, neck stiffness and a purple rash which does not fade on pressure. Drowsiness progresses to coma if untreated. I would add to these an inability to do any task that involves co-ordination. Treatment of meningitis requires powerful antibiotics, plus other high-tech treatments depending on the stage of the illness. Apart from superb ITU care at Shrewsbury, my survival was also undoubtedly due to a lot of prayer; I really was not very well!

The vaccine: For travel, the combined ACW135Y vaccine is now recommended. A single injection gives immunity 5-10 days after the injection and lasts five years. Vaccination should be given at least two weeks prior to departure. If you are going to be in Saudi Arabia during the pilgrimage to Mecca (Hajj), vaccination against these meningitis strains and a certificate of vaccination are required for immigration.

Yellow Fever. Our friend the mosquito is involved in the spread of this virus, so read the advice on bite avoidance. The majority of cases of yellow fever occur in tropical Africa, although it exists in central and south America as well. Jungle and forested parts of these areas carry the greatest risk of infection.

Symptoms appear after three to six days. There are basically two stages of the disease, and 15% of those infected will proceed to the more serious second stage. The first stage will present with a sudden high fever, weakness and lethargy, headache, muscle pains and vomiting. These symptoms will resolve in about a week or so and will disappear without treatment. The second, more dangerous, stage appears after a one or two day abatement in the symptoms. Jaundice (yellowing of the skin) occurs and more sickness returns, followed by bruising, nosebleeds, reduced urine output and convulsions. At this stage one would be very sick indeed and about 50% of people with these symptoms will die. There is no specific treatment, but the second stage requires advanced life-support measures in hospital.

The vaccine: A single injection will give ten years of protection. There are only certain centres that can give the injection. A yellow fever certificate is the only official document required by the World Health Organisation (WHO) for international travel. Many countries make vaccination a condition of entry, so keep your vaccination certificate safe. Your research will tell you to which countries this applies.

Rabies. Rabies is a viral infection which affects the central nervous system, and is fatal once symptoms have developed. It is spread from a bite or scratch from an infected animal, so never stroke or pet animals in an endemic area – the disease exists in most countries outside the UK, but parts of the developing world are particularly high risk. Avoiding it is simple – don't get bitten. You also need to be very aware of animals acting out of character such as a wild fox walking towards you calmly like a pet dog. When I was teaching in an American camp, a racoon approached us in this manner. My colleague grabbed a gun and sent it to its maker, then buried it deeply and quickly; he said that it probably had rabies. Generally, animals will leave you alone if you leave them alone.

Symptoms appear from two weeks to a year after being bitten. They are malaise, headache, nausea, vomiting, diarrhoea, sore throat and aching muscles. In addition, signs of anxiety, aggression and agitation may start. Muscle spasms and a fear of water develop. Once the symptoms start there is no cure, and the victim will die in a particularly unpleasant manner. It is vital to avoid animals biting you in the first place, and should you be bitten use any possible means to stop the animal biting you again. This means killing it if necessary. Clean the wound rigorously, using alcohol or spirit, as this may kill the virus before it enters the body and may also stop other bugs from the animal getting into the wound. Don't close the wound, just put a dressing over it and seek urgent medical help. Apart from the follow-up rabies injections, you may require a tetanus booster and antibiotic cover as well as surgical closure of the wound.

The vaccine: We don't advise people going to mainland Europe or the USA to have a rabies jab, and yet the risk of disease exists in these countries. When deciding whether to be immunised or not, you need to look at the level of rabies in the countries you are visiting, how far you will be from good quality medical care, and whether your planned activities are likely to bring you into contact with animals. Cost should not come into your decision. The vaccine is expensive, but if you are going to be at risk and can't afford it, don't go. For full protection you will require three injections over a twenty-eight day period, which provides immunity for two years. Note that this vaccine only buys you time. If you are bitten you must still get medical attention as soon as possible, as you will require at least two more injections.

Hepatitis B. A sobering thought is that about two billion people world-wide are carriers of the Hepatitis B virus. It is endemic in Africa, South America, Eastern Europe and Southeast Asia. It is spread through infected blood and blood products, sexual intercourse, needle sharing or other invasive procedures such as ear piercing or tattooing with inadequately sterilised equipment. This is the same as for HIV, but Hepatitis B is a hundred times more infectious. To avoid it means avoiding the above situations (more on the sex issue later). If you are working in a healthcare environment you should always have the vaccination. However, you do not always know what you are going to encounter when travelling. The risk of being involved in an accident abroad is greater than that of contracting a tropical illness. Any traveller overseas who is involved in an accident or other medical emergency, especially where a blood transfusion is required, is at risk from Hepatitis B. Some Gap Year people I met in Africa, who were teaching in village schools, ended up working for a while in a local hospital and were expected at one stage to work in the operating theatre. My advice to them was not to do so, due to the risks involved. They diplomatically refused and worked elsewhere in the hospital. This illustrates why it may be worth considering the vaccine, although like the rabies vaccine it is not available on the NHS.

Symptoms can take between six weeks and six months to appear, and are similar to Hepatitis A, including loss of appetite, malaise, nausea, weight loss, aches and pains and abdominal discomfort. Jaundice then follows. These symptoms normally last a month, but (unlike Hepatitis A) 5-10% of adults become chronic carriers and approximately 25% of these carriers will die of liver cirrhosis or liver cancer. Hepatitis B needs long-term management by a specialist in liver diseases.

The vaccine: There is an effective vaccination that requires three injections. Ideally, the first two injections take place a month apart, with the next one six months later. For 'last minute' travellers an accelerated course with a later booster can be used.

Tuberculosis (TB). This bug can affect any part of the body, but most commonly affects the lungs. A third of the world's population is infected with TB, and it is on the increase, with more deaths in sub-Saharan Africa from TB than malaria. Part of this increase is due to HIV infection and the resulting lack of immunity. It is spread through droplet infection from infectious people coughing or sneezing, or by drinking unpasteurised milk. Prolonged exposure is normally needed to contract the disease, such as living in overcrowded conditions or living closely with a high-risk group. The risk to travellers is generally low, but long-term travellers (over 3 months) to a country with a lot of TB, those planning to live and work in deprived communities, or travellers who are run down through bad diet or ill health may be more susceptible.

If you contract TB it's not something you will instantly know about. Symptoms can take months or years to appear, and when the lungs are affected these include shortness of breath, a cough (which often produces blood-stained sputum), weight loss, poor appetite, fevers and night sweats. Specialist medical treatment is required to treat TB, including many months of antibiotics.

The vaccine: The vaccine is commonly known as BCG and offers some protection from TB. If you have not had the vaccine your GP will normally arrange for a skin test to see whether you need it. Unless your skin test shows immunity it is sensible to be vaccinated for travel to most parts of the world. Booster doses are not recommended by the World Health Organisation (WHO). Remember, as with most vaccines, the protection is not 100%, so if you develop symptoms seek medical advice.

Japanese B encephalitis. Mosquitoes spread this one, so keep yourself protected against the little beasties and the vaccine won't even have to do its job. The risk of Japanese encephalitis is low for most travellers to the Far East and Southeast Asia, but varies with the seasons, type of accommodation and duration of exposure. It is endemic where pig farming takes place and in wet rural areas such as rice fields where mosquitoes flourish. The riskiest time is during and just after the wet season. Symptoms include vomiting, headache and fever; a stiff neck may occur along with photophobia (intolerance to light) and children may fit. These symptoms are similar to meningitis, cerebral malaria and cerebral oedema from high altitude sickness, because they all result from swelling of the brain. There is no specific treatment, but hospital care is needed due to the severity of the symptoms. In parts of Scandinavia, Central and Eastern Europe, another form of encephalitis called **tick-borne encephalitis** is prevalent in late spring and summer. As its name suggests, it is spread by ticks, and people who are thinking of camping or working in forested areas in these seasons should consider vaccination.

The vaccine: Three doses of vaccine are required, and give 90% protection. The Japanese B vaccine is not licensed in the UK as it is not generally recommended for travellers. However, it is available on an individual basis if your trip involves travel for over a month to rural areas where the disease is prevalent, during or just after the wet season.

Cholera. This is another disease transmitted by contaminated food and drink. Epidemics occur periodically in the developing world, and the disease is endemic in parts of Africa and Southeast Asia. It causes diarrhoea, which may be mild, but in some cases can be severe and life threatening. Vaccination is recommended for those working with refugees and in disaster relief situations, as the chances of epidemics occurring are far higher in these circumstances. It may be appropriate for some other travellers, particularly if there has been an outbreak of the disease in places you are planning to visit.

*The vaccine***:** This is given by mouth in two doses, at least a week apart, and lasts for two years.

DISEASES CARRIED BY INSECTS

Many travellers will venture into tropical parts of the world, where there is the risk of disease from insects. Malaria is the most well-known disease carried by insects, but there are others such as dengue fever, yellow fever and Japanese B encephalitis (described above). I could go on to discuss more exotic-sounding diseases, but this is not a tropical disease textbook. To avoid getting any of the above requires a four-pronged approach, which can be nicely summed up by ABCD:

A Awareness. Have an awareness of the disease risks from insects in the areas you plan to visit.
B Bites. Don't get bitten. In other words, protect yourself, using sensible clothing and insect repellent.
C Carry on taking the tablets. If it is available, take the appropriate prophylactic medication or make sure you have had the necessary vaccination to deal with the disease. It is vital that antimalarials are taken for the prescribed length of time – which

can be some weeks after the trip has finished or you have left the malarial zone.

D Diagnose. Recognise that you are not well so that you can get treatment.

Malaria

This is the one disease most people think about when they go to tropical countries. It is a big killer, with one to two million deaths per year in Africa alone, and up to 500 million cases per year worldwide. This means that the disease is likely to be present in most of the developing world, and so it is very important to put in place measures to protect yourself. Remember that if you protect yourself from mosquito bites you are also protecting yourself from many other diseases as well as malaria.

Malaria is carried by the Anopheles mosquito, which bites from dusk to dawn, so this is the time to take precautions – such as insect repellent and covering exposed skin with long clothing. These mosquitoes are particularly keen on wet, low-lying, humid areas, with still water being a particularly good breeding ground. There are two versions of the disease – the first type is potentially fatal and the second one is very unpleasant. The very unpleasant category has three variations on a theme.

The potentially fatal form of malaria is called *P. (Plasmodium) falciparum*. It can cause severe anaemia, convulsions, liver and kidney failure, and coma. This is referred to as 'malignant malaria' or more commonly 'cerebral malaria'.

The very unpleasant type takes three forms: *P. vivax, P. ovale* and *P. malariae*. The symptoms of these are fever, rigors (high temperature with violent shivering), headache, nausea and vomiting. These forms are known as 'benign malaria'.

In the early stages you will be unable to differentiate between benign and cerebral malaria, and both need treating anyway. Unfortunately, these symptoms mimic other conditions as well.

Awareness of the danger. Malaria is a disease of low-lying areas and is not supposed to be found above 5000ft, although I came across it at a height above this in Uganda. Obviously, the 'mozzies' there have not been reading the books! Your research should show you the high-risk places. You will still need to take your antimalarial medication as you travel between areas where malaria is endemic, but will not need to take other precautions if you are in an area free from mosquitoes and other biting insects. In areas where the little beasties are biting, protection using clothing and repellents is absolutely essential.

Avoiding being bitten. You have to get bitten to get malaria (or any other insect-carried disease, for that matter). Clothing and insect repellent play a key role here, because if you wear the appropriate clothing to cover exposed skin, use insect repellent, and avoid going out when the mosquitoes are most active, you are much less likely to get bitten. It stands to reason that if you wander around in a swimming costume at night, in an area full of mosquitoes, you are at a significant risk of being bitten by an infected mosquito. Your clothing should be loose fitting and cover your arms and legs. Wearing long ankle socks or tucking your trousers into your socks is a very good idea, as your ankles might otherwise be exposed when you sit down. A lot of travelling trousers now have draw cords or Velcro around the bottom of the legs which can help to prevent bites. When mosquitoes are around, women should opt for trousers instead of skirts. Mosquito nets and clothing can be soaked in permethrin, which will significantly discourage mosquitoes from visiting you. This is particularly worth doing if you are trekking in jungles, or in areas infested by ticks or sandflies.

Insect repellents

These have a vital role to play in your war against insect bites. The most common active ingredient is DEET, which comes in various strengths. The lowest effective strength for adults is 30%, and this should provide protection for 4 to 6 hours. Periodically, the media stirs up stories about how harmful it may be to your skin, but malaria is a lot more harmful and DEET-based repellents have been used for years. If you have any doubt, try it before you go. If your skin does react, there are alternatives available.

You only need to apply the repellent to exposed skin. Be careful how you apply it to your face, avoiding your mouth and eyes. If you are using a spray, spray the repellent onto your hand first and then apply it to your face using your fingers. You do not need to apply the repellent heavily. Avoid putting it on open cuts or wounds.

Sleeping

As the critical time for being bitten is from dusk until dawn, you need to consider your sleeping arrangements, securing the environment so that the mosquitoes can't get near you. The ways of doing this are as follows:

- Use a permethrin-coated mosquito net. Nets, when available in the developing world, are notorious for having holes in them, so always take your own.
- Make sure the net is tucked under your mattress. Some nets come with attachment kits, but it is a good idea to take items such as extra cord, hooks and long thumb tacks.
- Avoid sleeping against your mosquito net.
- Reimpregnate the net with permethrin every six months.
- Try to make sure you use a screened room, and make sure the screens fit well and stay shut.

- Spray insect repellent around the room and use insect repellent coils.
- If there is an air conditioning system, use it, as the cold inhibits mosquito activity.

Preventive medication

Despite all your best efforts to stop insects biting you, you may not be 100% successful, so we need to think about the next line of defence.

This boils down to taking medication that will destroy the malaria parasite when it's in your body. A key point to remember here is that no anti-malarial drug is 100% effective. Depending on what you take and where you are, the drugs are somewhere between 50% and 90% effective.

With regard to your anti-malarial, consider the following: The malaria parasites in certain areas have built up a resistance to some anti-malarial drugs. When choosing what drug to take, check up-to-date information. Listen to your travel health advisor or practice nurse, but do your own research as well, so that you can make an informed decision. The web addresses at the end of the book will help. Some drugs are only licensed for use for a limited period, although if your doctor is agreeable they may be prescribed for a longer period. All drugs have side effects and contra-indications which need to be considered, especially with regard to any pre-existing medical conditions you may have. Some anti-malarial drugs are extremely expensive, and none are available on the NHS.

The malaria parasite travels through the body in several stages. It is still active for a month while it goes through the liver, and is only destroyed by your medication when it comes back into the blood stream. It's for this reason that it is essential you take your anti-malarials for the prescribed amount of time after you leave the malarious area. After all, it only takes a few seconds to take the tablet, but getting malaria, particularly the cerebral type, will affect you and the people who have to look after you for a lot longer. Most anti-malarials require you to take them for four weeks after leaving a malarious area. The exception is Malarone, which is taken for one week, as it attacks the parasite in the liver as well as in the blood. One of the main reasons people succumb to malaria is that they stop taking their medication early. This is not an option if you want to avoid the disease. You also need to take the medication at the same time each day for it to be effective.

Below is a basic overview of the various anti-malarial drugs available at the time of writing. Generic (chemical) names are given first, trade names in parentheses. There is an issue with some of the newer drugs, which are only licensed for a certain length of time. Having said that, there is a lot of experience with longer use and your GP may allow you to have a longer prescription as long as you are aware it is prescribed outside the terms of the manufacturer's licence.

Chloroquine (Avloclor or Nivaquine). This drug has been available for a long time but in various places, principally sub-Saharan Africa, the malaria parasite has developed resistance to it. Two tablets are taken weekly. As with all drugs, there are potential side effects, but the only really common one is a minor stomach upset on the day you take it, minimised by taking it after food. If you have a history of epilepsy or are taking anti-epilepsy drugs you should take advice, as chloroquine is not normally recommended. You should start to take the tablets one week before your departure and continue for four weeks after leaving the malarious area.

Proguanil (Paludrine). Two tablets are taken daily. Mild stomach upset may be an issue and mouth ulcers can occur, more commonly if combined with chloroquine. In a similar way to chloroquine, resistance has developed to this drug and it is rarely used alone. The combination of proguanil and chloroquine has been used extensively in the past, but the areas of the world where this combination is still first choice are becoming limited due to the development of drug resistance. However, if other drugs are unsuitable it may still be used even in these areas; bite prevention is even more important when this is the case.

Mefloquine (Lariam). This is a very effective drug, and only needs to be taken once a week. Unfortunately, reports of neuropsychiatric side effects have made it less popular, although these have undoubtedly been over-emphasised by the media. Scientific evidence is more varied. Many studies have shown it to be well tolerated, but one study reported that 25% of people taking it said they had vivid dreams, panic attacks or depression in some form or another, although only a small percentage suffered in a very severe fashion. So what should you do if this tablet is otherwise right for you? I would suggest trying the tablet for a couple of weeks before it is really needed – in this way if you do have problems you can stop taking it and obtain an alternative before you go, so your holiday is not affected. You should not take it if you have had depression, other psychiatric illness or epilepsy, or if these conditions affect close blood relatives.

Proguanil with Atovaquone (Malarone). This is a new combination tablet for malaria prevention, although the drugs in it have been around for a while. Because it came into use recently, limited evidence is available regarding side effects, particularly in the long term. Studies so far indicate that it is very effective and has few reported side effects. It has to be taken for only two days before entering and one week after leaving the infected area, as opposed to a week before and four weeks after with other drugs. If you are taking tetracycline (a common antibiotic for acne), be aware that the protection offered by Malarone may be reduced. As always, you must concentrate on not letting mosquitoes bite you in the first place. The two problems with Malarone are that it is very expensive, and at present in the UK it is only licensed for one month's usage although it can be prescribed for longer periods at your GP's discretion. For short trips to high risk areas I would suggest it is the best drug to use, although the price may be prohibitive for a longer duration.

Doxycycline. It is strange, but this basic antibiotic is an effective anti-malarial. It is very popular with long-term Gap Year travellers as it is cheaper than Malarone and effective. It does, however, have side effects, including sun sensitivity, diarrhoea and thrush. I have yet to meet a traveller who does not want to go out in the sun, so bear this in mind!

Heartburn may result from taking the capsule on an empty stomach or lying down too soon after taking it. Take it standing up and wash it down with lots of water. The drug must not be used in pregnancy or if you are allergic to tetracycline antibiotics. Doxycycline may reduce the effectiveness of the oral contraceptive pill so take other precautions if you want to avoid pregnancy.

Malaria prevention: key points

To reduce your risk of getting malaria, remember these basic points:

1. Stop the insects biting you.
2. Take advice from a GP, practice nurse or travel clinic specialist with access to the latest information on which drugs are effective for your destination.
3. Take your malaria tablets for the prescribed length of time after you have left the area where malaria may be present.

If you don't heed this advice, the memories you have from your trip may not be the ones you dreamt about – you have been warned! Mike told me how it all went wrong for him:

> *Having felt sick on Lariam on a previous trip, when it came to getting anti-malarial tablets for a holiday in the Gambia, I decided not to take the tablets. During my holiday two*

ladies were flown home suffering from malaria, and still I didn't take any notice. I was adamant that I was going to enjoy the holiday, and suffer any consequences. Also I had an air-conditioned room, which was supposed to minimise the appearance of mosquitoes. Suffice to say, during a hot trip through a swamp in the Gambia, I was bitten. In the whole of the two-week holiday, I was bitten once, by one lonely mosquito. I thought nothing of it.

Five days after I returned from my trip, I cycled into work as usual, but felt awful, as if I was coming down with flu. I had a headache, and aches and pains all over. I felt better, then worse, over the next two days, but all the time I had a thumping headache which would not go away. I had arranged to meet a work colleague to hand over a project whilst I recovered. On the train into London I thought I was going to pass out, and when my friend arrived he thought I ought to go straight to a doctor, and led me to a private-paying medical centre in Central London. My symptoms were diagnosed as an infection of the inner ear, hence the temperature, headaches, and lack of balance. Some antibiotics were prescribed, which I picked up immediately and I took a taxi home.

Two days later, my girlfriend took me to the local hospital as I was making no sense at all, and was not able to keep any food down. After a desperate seven-hour wait in A&E, the doctors reported that I had a severe case of falciparium malaria – the most serious form of the disease. I was rushed to Intensive Care where they pumped my body with quinine to combat the parasites in the blood. The doctors were concerned as 11% of my blood was now parasites, and the quinine could give me liver or heart failure. It was a long night for my girlfriend and my family, but I was for the most part unaware of the problem.

The drugs worked and I was moved to a ward for a week, until my fluctuating temperature stopped going off the scale. I lost 16 pounds during those two weeks, and, although I still had the remnants of a tan, when I next saw my face, I hardly recognised the smile. It was a further six weeks until I felt fit enough to return to work.

Diagnosing and treating malaria

Despite taking all the above precautions, you may still get malaria. It is much less likely, but it's still a possibility as nothing can be made risk-free. The timeframe we are interested in is anything up to a year after you have potentially been exposed, with a particular focus on the first three months. The symptoms you should watch out for include:

- Flu-like symptoms, including aching muscles and joints
- Headache
- Sickness
- Fever
- Diarrhoea and vomiting

If you get these symptoms while travelling, get to medical aid as soon as possible. There are self-test kits available these days and it is possible to be given self-treatment kits as well. These might be worth having if you are likely to be isolated in a high risk area, and more than 24 hours from medical help, but most back-country hospitals in these areas will be able to test and treat appropriately for malaria. Studies have also shown that standby treatment is often used incorrectly, and any drugs provided need to be adjusted for the location you are in and the preventive tablets you are taking, on an individual basis. If you are back home and these symptoms occur, you must let the doctor or nurse know that there might be a risk of malaria – if they don't know you have been travelling, it may not be considered.

STOMACH AND BOWEL PROBLEMS

When travelling, a common subject for discussion is the state of one's bowels. Sickness is less common, although the same precautions apply to both diarrhoea and to vomiting (D&V). Travellers' diarrhoea (TD) is not solely the domain of the backpacker, as people on a package tour can also be susceptible, but the good news is that if you follow some common-sense guidelines, you'll significantly reduce the risk of an upset stomach.

Some travellers and authors offer advice about eating and drinking which I don't find particularly practical to follow, such as 'cook it, boil it, peel it or forget it'. Not only do these restrictions make for a pretty boring trip, but they are almost impossible to adhere to. I shall discuss in this section how to reduce the risk, through good personal hygiene, group hygiene and watching what you drink and eat. If this all sounds a bit too much hassle, remember that you already do this at home; it's just that when you're travelling you need to be more aware of these issues, but it will soon become second nature.

Hygiene

This is simply washing your hands when you have been to the toilet, as most of the food poisoning bugs are spread by dirty hands (the faecal-oral route).

It's easy enough to wash your hands if you're staying in hotels, backpacker lodges, guesthouses and so on, but what about when you are camping out in the wilderness? There might be basic long drop type facilities or it may be just a bush. As you work your way back from the toilet late at night, washing your hands may be the last thing on your mind. But do it! Simply grab your water bottle and give your hands a quick wash and rinse making sure you don't touch the mouth of the water bottle. It may be useful to take a supply of wet wipes or antibacterial hand gel. It's really basic hygiene but if you ignore it, you could ruin your adventure.

When cooking food the same rule applies – wash your hands before you prepare anything. There are likely to be more bugs around in the developing world, and your body will not be used to them, so you do need to be more vigilant. It's not a lot of effort and the results are worth it. If someone has D&V then don't let them near the food preparation area until at least 24 hours (ideally 48 hours) after their stomach has returned to normal.

At a base camp, even if it's only for a few days, dig a latrine or make sure everyone buries their waste completely. The toilet area should be well away from the cooking area and the water supply. Make a bowl out of polythene (use your initiative) so that people can wash their hands when they leave the toilet, or leave a water bottle and soap there.

The importance of personal hygiene cannot be overstated. Outdoor Experience instructor Bob Handley, a consultant trauma surgeon who has been a doctor for the British Antarctic Survey, says: 'It is the most important aspect of travel health and wilderness medicine. It's not glamorous but it is very important.'

WATER

When out and about on your travels it is essential to maintain good levels of hydration. Individual needs vary at any given time, depending on what you are doing and where you are. If you do become dehydrated you may feel ill or develop a headache – it feels like a hangover because that's what a hangover is, dehydration. It is unpleasant and unnecessary, and will make your trip less enjoyable. You are also more likely to make mistakes and bad decisions if you're not feeling well. More importantly, dehydration combined with working hard in a hot or humid environment can lead to heat exhaustion and heat stroke, which can have very serious consequences. These are discussed further in chapter nine, Surviving In Adverse Environments.

So how do you know if you are dehydrated? Is there a rule of thumb you can use? Firstly, thirst is not a reliable indicator of dehydration and neither are dried and cracked lips, which may simply be sunburnt. The only sure indicator of whether you are drinking enough water is the amount and colour of your urine. You should be able to fill and empty your bladder at least two or three times a day, producing clear, colourless or pale yellow urine. If you don't urinate this frequently, or if your urine is darker in colour, then you need to increase your intake of water. Advising you to drink x amount of litres per day is not a good idea, as individual requirements vary so much. If you are hiking with a pack in a hot, humid jungle, your daily water requirement will be much greater than if you are resting in a drier climate.

Having established that maintaining an appropriate level of fluid intake is important, how do you go about doing this? Getting water is not usually a problem, but it may contain nasty bugs. It is essential that you understand the potential danger and buy soft drinks or bottled water, or purify water yourself before drinking or brushing your teeth with it. Diarrhoea is the most common problem from contaminated water, though more serious infections can occur. If possible, be aware of where the water has come from. Wells that are properly built and capped or high mountain springs without animal contamination are often safe sources of water, though it is hard to be sure every time. While many travellers manage without carrying much equipment for treating water, if in doubt it is safest to use one of the methods discussed below.

Bottled water is a relatively cheap and easily obtainable source of safe drinking water in developing countries. Check that the seals on the bottles are unbroken, as it has been known for locals to refill empty bottles with unsafe tap water and sell them. Carbonated drinks are often available, even in less well-travelled areas, and if these are a well-known brand with the 'fizz' intact they are likely to be safe. If bottled water is not available (and it's surprising how readily you can get hold of it, even in isolated villages) you'll need a quick and practical way to purify potentially unsafe water for drinking, cooking and personal hygiene. Micro-organisms can be removed by filtering, boiling or chemically treating the water.

Filtration. Filtration may be used before boiling or chemical treatment for extra safety. The process removes any sediment from the water, making it look better and reducing the amount of chemicals needed to purify it. Some filters can remove micro-organisms as small as viruses, if used correctly, and some also contain an iodine compound that kills any organisms that do get through, without making the water taste too different. There are many types and makes available at a variety of prices, so it's a case of asking in good outdoor shops, looking in catalogues and checking what's around on the internet.

Boiling. Raising water temperature above 85°C (185°F) kills most pathogens within a few minutes, so all pathogens should be killed in the time it takes for water to be heated to boiling point (100°C/212°F at sea level). For extra safety, water should be boiled vigorously for one minute, or at altitude for an extra minute or two, as water boils at a lower temperature. Tea, coffee and soup can usually be considered safe, even in remote areas, because the water has been boiled. The problems with boiling as a purification technique are the inconvenience and the need for a source of heat. Theoretically, the caffeine in tea and coffee can act as a diuretic, but travellers the world over drink copious amounts without any ill effect.

Chemical treatment. Various chemical purification treatments are available. Iodine is generally very effective and has been used for years. It is supplied as tablets, crystals or tinctures. It can impart a slightly unpleasant taste and colour to the water, may stain clothing and skin during use and is harmful in overdose. Adding vitamin C or fruit drink powder to the water following iodine purification can improve its taste, but it inactivates any further iodine that is added. It should not be given to pregnant women or people who are allergic to iodine. A powder form of chlorine called Chloramine-T provides a cheap method of purifying large quantities of water. Water temperature, sediment loading and contact time all affect the effectiveness of chemical-based water purification treatments, which is why it is sensible to filter visibly contaminated water before adding chemical treatments.

Summary

Water is very important. Key points to remember are:

- Make sure you drink enough water.
- Buy safe water or purify it before use, and consider non-caffeinated soft drinks to maintain hydration.
- Avoid excessive consumption of alcohol or caffeine as these will dehydrate you.
- Have a good, one litre, metal water bottle for carrying water; these can take a battering without leaking.
- Choose a water purification method appropriate to the destinations you intend to visit, and obtain the necessary kit before departure.
- Carry a backup system, e.g. take chemicals as well as a filtration system.
- Avoid swimming in, or eating seafood from, potentially contaminated water.
- Avoid ice which could be made with contaminated water.

It is possible to travel into isolated developing-world environments without having to purify water; however, taking a purification system is highly recommended and will give you considerable peace of mind.

FOOD

How do you avoid dodgy food when travelling? What is the secret to being one of those people who return from their trip saying that, despite visiting the roughest destinations and eating all the local food, their stomachs were perfect? It's a combination of common sense, instinct and taking sensible precautions.

The key tips for significantly reducing the risk of Delhi belly are as follows:

- On arrival in a developing world area, try to keep to a bland diet for a day or two and keep your fluid intake up whilst you adjust to the environment. (Instantly trying out that local curry could be too much of an insult to your digestive system.) This will also give you time to find out the best (and safest) eating places.

- Food quality – order your food well done, as this is more likely to kill any nasties than if it is less well cooked. Fish will go off quickly, so eat it soon after it has been caught. If you are a long way from the sea, check that it is freshwater fish, and not seafish that has been transported a long distance. Be very wary of shellfish, as they filter large amounts of water; if they come from a polluted area this is not good news. Fruit is good for you, but it's best to eat fruit you have to peel.

- You may see bargain 'Chef's Specials' advertised. This can be good but could also mean, 'Yesterday's uneaten food that I want to get rid of. Don't worry about the flies that have been on it – I am sure they did not bring any bacteria with them.'

- If in any doubt about milk, boil it.

- Freshly-cooked food is usually less of a risk compared with buffet food or salads. Buffet food may have sat around for a long time, with the result that flies may well have got to it. Flies are equally at home on the local rubbish dump as they are on a nicely laid out buffet, so if it's a choice between that or something freshly cooked, choose the freshly cooked meal. Salads may have been washed in unsafe water; unless you can check this is not the case, it's best to avoid them.

- If a café or restaurant seems quiet it's probably best to avoid it; if it is popular it is probably okay. Ask around to find reliable and value for money eating places.

- Rice is a staple diet throughout the developing world, but avoid eating reheated rice as the bacteria it can harbour can cause severe D&V. The toxins may not even be destroyed by pressure cooking, so stick to freshly cooked rice.

- An awkward situation may arise when local people ask you to eat with them. This can be really difficult as you may not know the origins of the food, have doubts about its safety, or it may simply be something you don't like. Having said this, I have eaten some very good local food. Whatever you decide to do, be polite – personally I would usually accept the invitation and eat at least a small amount.

On my travels I have used the above guidelines and, other than the odd mild stomach upset, most of my fellow travellers and I have been fine. There are different strategies that you can employ; a technique that worked for me in big cities in India was to have one main meal a day at a reasonable hotel and to exist on snacks for the rest of the day. It was very hot at the time so we did not feel like eating during the day anyway. It seemed in the hotel's best interests to minimise the risk of food poisoning, so the staff were more likely to wash their hands and use reasonable water for washing food, etc. This worked and the food was good. For most of our time in Kashmir we ate superb, freshly cooked food on the houseboat. We ate street food in Thailand because we could watch it being cooked at very high temperatures and it looked (and tasted) very good!

At times (but not always) you may have to pay a small amount extra for your food. It may be a price worth paying to stay fit, healthy and able to enjoy your adventures. It is a false economy to save a few pence and end up stuck at a backpackers' lodge, reading about all the places you could go to if only you could move more than fifteen yards from the bathroom!

This is Andy and Sally's personal account of their recent trip to India:

Our gap year travel was not that time between school and university but between family holidays and Saga holidays. Our two sons were away at university; both had experienced travel and we wanted that same experience but with the rougher edges smoothed out. We chose India and we planned – we had almost as much fun looking on the internet, speaking to others who had made the same journey and pondering over maps, as we had on the holiday. We had the same passion for adventure and travel as the youngsters with the advantage of a little more cash (or less need to spend it purely on alcohol and entertainment). This meant we could stay in hotels: we chose hotels frequented by locals and by booking ahead we secured luxury hotels at a rate of 800-1400 rupees a night (£13-£20, not much more expensive than hostels run for the use of Europeans) for the two of us with breakfast. The continental option meant it might be necessary to have lunch, but the Indian breakfast would certainly last until supper with the odd banana en-route.

Visiting the numerous street markets, we were tempted by the food on display but unless we could peel it or unwrap it we refrained. One embarrassing moment was when a market stall holder, seeing us wondering what a particular strange vegetable was, took it off display, washed it in a nearby bucket of water and handed it to us to try. We had to pretend to eat it so as not to offend. We soon discovered that hotels and restaurants extruded the same wonderful smells, with the meal being served in a more congenial setting – often a palace that was too big and expensive for the current Maharajah of the area. We had a Delhi belly-free holiday by drinking bottled water only (even when cleaning teeth or swallowing malaria-prevention medication), eating in restaurants and avoiding meat. We avoided the meat out of choice, as it was often served on the bone and we were not sure of its origin. It certainly would not be the one meat that is safe to eat if undercooked ...beef from the sacred cow.

Before we set out, an Indian friend had told us how to open a conversation and how to finish it, a quote that we were to remember frequently. By talking to local people we learnt so much more than the guide books told us about the country, but once started we could be sitting for many hours talking!

Treating travellers' diarrhoea

If you have travellers' diarrhoea, it normally resolves within three days without intervention. If you don't have a high fever, severe abdominal pain and are not passing bloody diarrhoea, give it up to a week to go. If you have these worrying symptoms at any time, or if it has not gone after a week, then you should obtain a medical opinion. Occasionally antibiotics are needed, but the vast majority of cases of diarrhoea resolve without them; indiscriminate use can make diagnosis difficult and increase bacterial resistance. You need to maintain your fluid intake during the episode and can eat if you feel like it, but keep it bland.

It is possible to take tablets that 'bung you up'. These are only advisable in certain circumstances; for example, when you are going on a long journey which can't be rescheduled. They slow down the bowel's movement by up to 80%, but should not be used if fever or bloody diarrhoea is present. Your pharmacist will recommend which one to take.

PRE-EXISTING MEDICAL CONDITIONS

There are many areas that could be considered here but the main ones are asthma, epilepsy, diabetes, dietary conditions and allergies. Your GP or hospital consultant may well be required to give advice. Broadly speaking, I am of the view that with the application of some common sense most people should be able to have a great adventure, even if it means having a slightly less ambitious plan.

People with well-controlled epilepsy or asthma should be absolutely fine, as long as a sufficient amount of medication can be carried. Take plenty in reserve, and don't forget to carry some in your hand luggage. Your doctor or pharmacist should be able to check which countries have your medication, in case you run out or you are going for such a long period of time that carrying the full supply is not practical.

Conditions like diabetes can be more variable and challenging. Diabetes UK has an enormous amount of information on travelling with diabetes and, depending on your proposed trip and the type and severity of your diabetes, your GP or consultant will be able to advise on what is practical. Special containers are available to ensure safe carriage and storage of drugs, especially insulin. Other conditions such as coeliac disease, inflammatory bowel disease or severe allergies will also need advice from your GP or specialist, together with an assessment of your itinerary.

Make sure you obtain a doctor's note confirming your requirements for medication and that it is stored in a suitable container. If travelling with friends, they could carry some of your spare medication. Always keep some with you, in case your main luggage goes walkabout. It is a good idea to keep a note of your condition and medication in your wallet, because if you are too ill to tell someone what is wrong, medical staff are likely to check there for information. You can also get 'SOS' bracelets and necklaces.

You will already have an awareness of your condition and how it affects you. With common sense and sensible planning, you should be able to have an enjoyable and fulfilling adventure.

DEEP VEIN THROMBOSIS (DVT)

The risk of DVT from flying has become quite topical in the media. DVT, or a blood clot in the leg, can travel to the lungs with potentially fatal consequences (this is called a pulmonary embolus or PE). The same argument could theoretically be applied to long journeys on all forms of transport, as it is thought that inactivity is important in the formation of these clots. There is an excellent government website on travel and DVT, best found by going to www.dh.gov.uk and searching for DVT. The risk is generally very low, but may be slightly higher in those over 40 years of age, and is greater in people who:

- Have had blood clots already
- Have a strong family history of blood clots or an inherited clotting tendency
- Are suffering from, or have had recent treatment for, cancer
- Are being treated for heart failure and circulation problems
- Have had recent surgery, especially on the hips or knees
- Are pregnant or have had a baby very recently
- Are taking the contraceptive pill or HRT

Those at increased risk should take specific advice from their doctor. Listed below is general advice to reduce the risk of DVT when flying:

- Get comfortable in your seat and recline as much as possible

- Bend and straighten your legs, feet and toes while seated, and press the balls of your feet down hard against the floor to increase the blood flow in your legs
- Do upper body and breathing exercises to improve circulation
- Take occasional short walks around the cabin, whilst cruising at altitude
- Take advantage of refuelling stopovers where it may be possible to get off the plane and walk about
- Drink plenty of water
- Avoid alcohol, which in excess leads to dehydration and immobility
- Avoid taking sleeping pills

The danger signs which might indicate DVT include swelling, pain, tenderness and redness at the back of the leg below the knee. This usually, though not always, affects only one leg. This complaint may develop during the journey but more commonly happens hours or even days later. Mild ankle swelling is normal after flying, so should not be confused with possible DVT. The pain may be made worse by bending the foot upward towards the knee. Occasionally, the first sign of a problem is when an embolus occurs. This rare complication causes breathlessness, chest pain and, in severe cases, collapse. If you are concerned that you might have DVT or PE, get medical help as soon as possible.

WOMEN'S HEALTH

There are additional issues which women face and Sandra Grieve, a highly experienced travel health nurse, has written the following section:

Women have always been intrepid travellers, but it is only recently that gender differences in terms of travel have been addressed. Gender and age issues are important if travel and disease risks are to be identified and prevented. This book is aimed at fit, active people but there are a few considerations you should make before setting off into the unknown. I often say to women travellers that there is no Boots the Chemist at the foot of Mount Kenya, so think about what you are likely to need and take it with you. The sections on first aid/travel survival kits are comprehensive, so use those as a base and add personal preferences. If you are pregnant or planning a pregnancy, other issues come into play, such as immunisations and malaria prophylaxis, and specialist advice should be sought. A few common issues to consider are:

Culture/clothing. Women may be flouting convention merely by being in a given country and indulging in activities seen as male territory. Keep a low profile, blend in with the locals and avoid eye contact with men, which may be misread as 'I fancy you'. Sunglasses are a great way to limit this problem. I know of single women who 'invent' a husband and wear a wedding band to avoid unwelcome male attention. Do not dress in a provocative manner in areas where this would be inappropriate.

Lack of facilities. Women tend to be more aware of hygiene standards and facilities abroad, and recognise that they are unlikely to be like those at home. Lack of comfort breaks and privacy can be difficult for Western travellers to come to terms with, but squatting in the bush may be the only option. Access to clean water for personal hygiene may be limited, but it is important to keep skin clean and avoid sores and chafing, especially in tropical countries. Urinary infections and vaginal thrush are common in these situations, so ask your doctor to prescribe an antibiotic if you are a known sufferer. Carry wet wipes for toilet purposes. Help yourself by reading and enquiring about likely facilities available in the country you will visit.

Menstruation. Irregular menstruation is common in women travellers. Sometimes periods stop altogether during long trips, but although this may be convenient, consider whether pregnancy is a possibility. Excessive activity and stress of travel can aggravate already painful periods, so carry a favourite painkiller. Tampons, sanitary products and toilet rolls are not necessarily available in many developing countries, although guidebooks may give you an indication of availability. Disposal bags and wet wipes are easy to pack into small spaces. It may be worth asking your doctor how, by prescribing the oral contraceptive pill or adapting the current regime, menstruation can be postponed.

Fluid Retention. Long periods of inactivity and sitting during travel can lead to swollen feet and legs. This may increase the risk of DVT, especially for women who fall into a higher risk category (as listed above). If fluid retention is a recurrent problem, see your doctor. Simple exercises, moving around whenever possible and wearing suitable comfortable clothing and shoes will aid general circulation.

Contraception. There are several forms of contraception but the oral contraceptive pill (OCP - the Pill) is a popular method. Consider your itinerary, type of travel (remoteness) and length of trip before deciding on the best option for you. Your GP or family planning clinic will discuss your needs.

A few useful notes:

- **Crossing time zones.** Remember to take the pill every 24 hours – even if it means setting your alarm clock to remind you. Failure to do so may result in ovulation or breakthrough bleeding.
- **Forgotten pills.** Take the missed pill as soon as you realise and the next one at the usual time. Use other contraception methods for the rest of the month.
- **Taking antibiotics.** Some antibiotics may reduce the efficacy of the pill. Use another form of contraception as a precaution.

- **Unprotected sex.** This can lead to sexually transmitted infections (STIs) or unplanned pregnancy. Avoid casual sex and use condoms. The morning after pill may not be available and may be illegal in some countries.
- **D&V interferes with absorption of the pill.** If vomiting occurs within a few hours of taking the pill, take another. With travellers' diarrhoea, continue as usual but use condoms.
- **Mefloquine.** If mefloquine is prescribed for malaria prophylaxis avoid conception for 3 months after the last pill.
- **Supplies.** Take enough supplies of pills and condoms and follow the manufacturer's guidelines on storage and usage, especially in the tropics.

Pregnancy. If pregnant, consider the activities and risks the trip will bring. Can the trip be postponed? The second trimester (14-24 weeks) is considered to be the safest time if travel is unavoidable, as earlier there is a risk of miscarriage and the theoretical risk from immunisations; later there are risks to the developing foetus from disease. Think realistically about increased fatigue, the heat, lack of medical facilities and what activities you might not be able to participate in. When you consider all of these things during the planning stage, is it still worth travelling? Take good medical advice before you answer that! If an unplanned pregnancy occurs during travel, stop and consider the options. Getting home may be the best solution.

Safety and security. This is covered in chapter six. Many women do travel alone, but people in some countries see this as a peculiar act. In many countries women do not enjoy the personal freedom that those of us in the West take for granted. Take advice on the country you plan to visit and whether or not it is a good idea to go there alone.

TEETH

There are two aspects to caring for your teeth – prevention of problems and what to do should problems arise.

Prevention of tooth or gum problems is straightforward. Go to your dentist about twelve weeks before departure and have a check up. This will give the dentist plenty of time to do fillings and other toothy-type stuff. Make sure to mention that you are going travelling, as the dentist may decide to treat teeth rather than monitoring for a few months more. If you have had a lot of specialist attention to your teeth, seek advice from your dentist as to what to do should any problems arise. Why ruin the experience of being in a beautiful tropical hideaway because you have a raging toothache or abscess? Get your teeth checked!

Whilst travelling, make sure that you maintain good oral hygiene – in other words, clean your teeth. This not only contributes to good oral health but also makes you feel good. Toothpaste is not essential, although it makes your mouth feel fresh. Take some dental floss with you – not only does it maintain dental hygiene, but it can also be used to hang mosquito nets.

If you have had your teeth properly checked you should avoid dental problems such as toothache and dental abscesses. Erosion of the tooth's enamel due to decay causes the nerve in the tooth to be exposed and hence brings on toothache. Left untreated, this can lead to the death of the nerve, which can ultimately mean an abscess will form. The first sign of trouble is a sensitivity to hot and cold, which does not settle. This means you will have to get your teeth looked at by a reputable dentist, which is not always easy in the developing world. As things deteriorate the pain will get worse and will not settle, particularly when eating. If this happens avoid very hot, cold or spicy food and drink, take pain relief tablets and wash your mouth out with warm salt water. It is possible to buy dental first aid kits to patch up a sore tooth as a first aid measure, but dentists do not generally recommend self-treatment.

A dental abscess can originate through a problem with a tooth or through gum disease. Symptoms are severe persistent pain, swelling of the gum, an unpleasant taste in the mouth and a swollen face. Abscesses can become very serious and can lead to a life-threatening infection. One of my sisters had a tooth abscess which led to a brain abscess a few days later. She made a full recovery, but only after six hours of emergency neurosurgery. Initial treatment of a tooth abscess involves the use of broad-spectrum antibiotics, as dentists cannot do much until the infection is brought under control.

Getting treatment abroad will involve you using your travel insurance, as emergency dental work is not cheap. The key feature of the dental section of travel health insurance is that it's for the 'relief of immediate pain'; it's not for cosmetic work such as broken crowns. Check when you take out your policy exactly what is covered, as not all policies include dental work and the amount covered varies.

EYE CARE

This section covers general eye care, issues relating to contact lenses or glasses, and snow blindness.

The main thing about eye care is to stop dust and grit getting into your eyes by wearing sunglasses in situations where this is likely to happen. Occasionally, you may get an infection, where you have a yellow discharge out of one eye. Many cases will get better on their own and will improve by bathing the eye with cooled boiled water. Avoid touching the other eye with the hand that has touched the infected one. If the white of the eye is particularly red and the discharge does not go, then antibiotic drops will be needed. If your eyesight is affected, apart from slight blurring from the discharge, seek medical advice urgently. You should seek medical advice sooner if you use contact lenses than if you don't, as these can predispose you to more severe infections.

If you wear glasses, take a spare pair. I have worn gas-permeable contact lenses for years and although I have had few problems, on the odd occasion that they have played up, I have really known about it. I would therefore advise you to take some glasses with you in case you need to give your eyes a rest. At least one spare pair of lenses and plenty of solutions are also required. These are not bulky and if you can't source any, you could try to have them posted to you. Make sure your contact lenses are suitable for your type of trip. Check with your optician, as some lenses require a lot of looking after. If you have any sort of eye infection, stop wearing your contact lenses immediately and, as mentioned above, if the eye becomes red and painful seek urgent medical advice.

One danger of travelling on snow fields or at high altitudes is snow blindness (sunburn of the cornea). It is excruciatingly painful and feels like having sandpaper rubbed into your eyes. The eyelids can become very swollen and it is debilitating. It is treated by putting a patch over the eye and, preferably, lubricating it with some form of eye drop. It is far more sensible to stop it happening in the first place, by wearing a pair of quality sunglasses with side patches or snow goggles which cut out 100% of the ultraviolet light. If you don't have any sunglasses, as an emergency measure you can make an eye patch with cloth or cardboard and cut a narrow slit in it.

SKIN CARE

We all like to get a tan as it makes us look good and feel good. The big difference on longer trips is that you will have longer to do this, so don't rush it. If you get it wrong you will be very sore, feel ill and possibly be a liability to your companions, not to mention the proven risk of skin cancer from long term over-exposure to the sun. To avoid getting burnt is really easy, but requires some self-discipline and common sense. This means not over-exposing yourself to the sun – particularly areas of the body not normally exposed – when it's at its strongest, say between 11am and 3pm. In the tropics the sun is more intense and you can get burnt even when there is cloud cover. I am not suggesting that you shouldn't go out but if it's really hot and sunny, especially if you are at high altitude, put plenty of cream on any exposed skin. Reapply regularly and make sure you use a high-protection factor (the absolute minimum is 15) which is waterproof, so it does not come off if you go swimming. Think about wearing a hat, and in the middle of the day keep a T-shirt on. If you do get burnt, cover up for a few days to let the skin heal. When you choose a sun cream, remember that the price does not necessarily reflect its quality.

Skin cancer is the most commonly diagnosed cancer, so do not ignore the risks. These are greater for those who are fair skinned and who burn or freckle easily. If you are sensible you will not have a problem.

You also need to bear in mind that various drugs, including the common anti-malarial doxycycline, can make your skin sensitive to the sun.

FIRST-AID (TRAVEL SURVIVAL) KITS

99.9% of the time you are only likely to need plasters from your medical kit, but you need to prepare for the 0.1% chance that things may be a bit more serious. The same principle applies in your car – you put a seat belt on just in case.

Your first-aid kit should be a travel survival kit, containing useful medical and non-medical items to help you to stay comfortable and safe. It is important for you to have one, even if you are going on some sort of organised trip, as this does not exclude you from the responsibility of having a kit that enables you to look after yourself. There is considerable peace of mind in knowing that you can treat your own blisters and have your own headache tablets, lip cream and the like.

When organising your travel survival kit, the main points to note are:

- It should be as compact as possible in a hard-wearing nylon bag. Dark nylon wash kit bags are useful as they do not attract attention and have lots of storage room.
- You must know exactly what's in the kit and how to use it.
- The contents should be specifically tailored to your requirements, taking into account geographical and activity considerations.

The contents of your travel survival kit can be divided into medical and non-medical items.

Medical items

If you go into outdoor shops you will find a plethora of travel medical kits that cater for pretty much every eventuality. All have their unique selling points explaining why you should buy them. It is important though that you understand what's in them. With a pre-packed kit, there is inevitably a bit of laziness and a tendency to think, 'I'm all right, I've bought a first-aid kit', and when you need to use it, it may not contain what you need. If you do buy a ready-made kit, decide if all the items are necessary. For instance, the kit may have scissors in it but you probably have those on your Swiss Army knife, so why take a second pair? You need to make sure you know how to use every item, and supplement the kit with extra medical and non-medical items, based on your own requirements.

Deciding what to take in your travel survival kit requires a bit of common sense risk analysis. You'll then need to head off to a chemist, outdoor shop or possibly the internet to buy the items.

Working out what items you need, and buying them, really helps you to value everything in your kit. What do I mean by risk analysis? If, for instance, I was going into the jungle, I might need the ability to stem a potentially life-threatening haemorrhage from a machete injury. For this environment, I would take two ambulance dressings (which have a large gauze pad with a bandage attached, enabling direct pressure to be put on a bleeding wound), and I would encourage colleagues to do likewise. If I was trekking to a high mountain peak, I would carry just one dressing, as machetes would not be used. Some years ago I went on a wilderness and caving expedition to the Norwegian Arctic. We thought it was likely to be wet, so my travel survival kit included a candle, a couple of solid fuel blocks, a lighter and some matches. All of these were used to create a very welcome fire from sodden wood in wet, wild and stormy conditions – this turned what could have been a miserable day into an adventure that was memorable for the right reasons.

Basic medical items you need to take are:

Plasters. You will probably need a lot, so take a variety of sizes plus a strip of wider plaster which you can cut to size.

Cleaning wipes. Anti-bacterial wipes are useful for cleaning small wounds. (Larger wounds should be cleaned with soap and cooled boiled water.)

Field/ambulance dressing. This is a gauze pad with a bandage sewn on, and is used to stop severe bleeding. These can be bought from army surplus stores or chemists.

Cotton wool. A few bits are useful, for nose bleeds, etc.

Roll of tape. Used for holding dressing pads or bandages in place. There are gentle types such as micropore or the stronger Elastoplast. If you are taking just one roll of tape, Elastoplast is more versatile.

Dressing pads. Take two or three gauze pads or dressings of different sizes, for more substantial grazes or cuts.

Surgical gloves. These should be considered essential as you may have to deal with someone else's body fluids whilst treating an injury. They can be bought from a chemist.

Bandages. You need a crepe bandage large enough for a sprained knee, ankle or wrist. It's best to take two, one 8cm wide and one 4cm wide. They can be used to make a sling, to bandage limbs together, provide compression in cases of very severe bleeding, or to hold together splints that you have made from a sleeping mat.

Triangular bandage. This is used as an arm sling or as a bandage when folded. Get a compressed one, as it is very compact.

Medication. Your local pharmacist will advise you on the best tablets to take with you. Areas you need to consider are:

- **Pain relief** such as ibuprofen and paracetamol.
- **Antihistamines** for bites, stings, allergies and itchy skin rashes.
- **Anti-diarrhoea tablets.** Guidelines for the use of these can be found under "Treating Travellers' Diarrhoea" in chapter four, "Staying Healthy."

Personal medication. If you are on any medication, you need to take a reserve supply; store some in your travel survival kit.

Antibiotics. These will not be needed by most travellers, but if you are likely to be exploring lots of isolated places in the developing world it may be worth carrying broad spectrum antibiotics. Being more than 72 hours from any sort of medical help is probably a good benchmark as to whether or not to consider them. Your GP is likely to be sympathetic to your request, but remember that the GP is responsible for the prescription whenever and wherever it is used, and will want to make sure that you understand when you should (and shouldn't) use them.

These prescriptions should not be issued by the NHS, so as with malaria tablets you will need to pay the market price. The antibiotics are prescribed for your personal use only – do not give them to anyone else, as they may have an allergy that could cause a severe reaction. If you start a course, you should take the tablets for the recommended number of days. Most infections get better without antibiotics, and you should not use them without a really good reason; but situations where they may (and *only* may) be required might include:

Diarrhoea - should you have severe diarrhoea for more than seven days, you may consider using them. However, if you have had it that long you should really be obtaining a medical opinion to make a diagnosis before treatment. Overuse of antibiotics for diarrhoea in places like Thailand has led to significant resistance, even to modern antibiotics.

Ear infection - most ear infections do not need antibiotics, but if you are prone to problems with your ears it may be worth taking them.

Urinary tract infection - some people, usually women, are prone to repeated bladder or kidney infections, and if this applies to you a standby course of treatment might be worth carrying.

Tooth abscess - very painful and nasty, as previously described.

Skin and soft tissue infections - cuts and bites can occasionally get infected, and in the unlikely event of a large wound or open fracture, where it might take some time to get to hospital, antibiotics might help to prevent wound infection.

If you are taking medication with you, ask your GP to write a letter confirming that the tablets are for your use and what they are for. This sorts out any issue with Customs and so on. I often think it is useful, if possible, to bury your travel survival kit deep in your bag, so that Customs officers are less likely to start going through it. It avoids hassle. It is worth mentioning that it is sometimes possible to get an emergency medical opinion by e-mail or satellite phone, which might be an option, particularly for organised projects.

Sterile supplies kits. These contain sterile needles, syringes, surgical stitches and drips (cannulae). They are for use in the unfortunate event of you requiring emergency medical treatment in a hospital that does not have sterile, single-use items available. You might want to pack this (and your dental kit, if you decide to take one) separately, as they are unlikely to be used and may get damaged as your travel survival pack will be opened frequently. It is worth getting a pre-packed and sealed kit, so it is clear that the syringes are not for illicit drug taking. Don't forget, you must not pack it in your hand luggage when flying, or it will be removed by airport security.

Non-medical items

There are lots of bits and pieces to be included here:

- **Nylon cord** - this has a multitude of uses
- **Candles and matches** - for power cuts or fire lighting
- **Spare batteries and bulb** - for your torch
- **Sewing kit** - hopeless in my hands, although I have sewn a rucksack strap back on using surgical nylon – and it was still going strong years later!
- **Lip cream** - get one with sun block
- **Safety pins** - have loads of uses. I have held sunglasses together with them, for example
- **Spare contact lenses and solutions** - or glasses if you wear them
- **Spare camera batteries**
- **Water purification tablets**

There seems to be a lot of stuff listed above, but it really can fit into a wash bag size container. You might also want to put a copy of your insurance details, emergency contact numbers and other useful information in it.

Having a travel survival kit is all well and good, but it is not much use unless you know how to use it. Chapter ten goes into more detail about wilderness first-aid. Don't be put off by this title. If you are in an isolated environment it doesn't matter whether you end up putting a bandage around a friend's sprained ankle, look after someone with an upset stomach, put a plaster on the knee of a youngster you are teaching in South America or deal with something more serious – you are practising wilderness first-aid.

Backpacking - Abel Tasman, New Zealand

Waterfall - Uganda

Does it get any better than this? (© Hugh Matthews)

A different way to boil an egg

Dal Lake, Kashmir

Tea in the Himalayas

Buying bread in rural village - Northern India

Sleeping on the beach - Thailand

Local entrepreneurs - Kathmandu

Lunchtime afloat in India

Chilling out in Australia - waiting for floods to subside

Personally, I would have used this water for tea!

Queen Elizabeth National Park - Uganda

Evening in Africa

Well earned drink in the Himalayas

Excellent street food - Thailand

Market Traders - Algeria

The recovery position

Chatting with the locals in the Rift Valley, Kenya

Skiing - Washington State, USA

Sunrise, summit ridge - Mount Kenya

5

ON YOUR WAY

THE AIRPORT

The big day has arrived, the jabs have been done, the kit is well thought out and packed and you're on your way. You've probably said a fair round of goodbyes and just want to get going, but you're also probably a bit (or maybe very!) nervous. This feeling is normal, so try not to worry – after all, you've got this book to refer to! In this step-by-step guide, I'm hoping to steer you through any problems you may encounter, and I make no apologies if some advice seems obvious – I want to provide a safety net for less well travelled readers.

Your first port of call shouldn't require you to delve into your travel survival kit, but you may need carefully chosen supplies to endure it – the airport! With the possibility of flight delays, you'll have to allow for the boredom factor – make sure you have something to read and enough local currency to buy refreshments. A Discman or similar may help to alleviate the boredom.

Generally, airports are pretty safe, but common sense should dictate that you look after your hand baggage and keep your wallet, passport and tickets secure. Since the World Trade Centre bombings on 11th September 2001, the regulations regarding hand baggage have been considerably tightened, so do not take anything that could be misinterpreted, particularly anything sharp or metal. You should not take photographs at an airport without checking that it is permitted – in many countries you will lose your camera if you are caught taking photos. Be aware that most airlines are enforcing rules on the size of hand baggage, to prevent people using more of the overhead locker space than they are entitled to. You do not need that much space to carry the essential hand luggage items.

With regards to the flight, just enjoy it (remember the advice about DVT in chapter four, Staying Healthy, but don't lose any sleep over it). As for being bumped up a class, it has not happened to me yet, but I live in hope.

ARRIVAL – CULTURE SHOCK

You've finally touched down in a foreign land! When you go through Customs and immigration, do not joke with them about anything at all, particularly anything to do with weapons or terrorism. Just smile sweetly and be nice.

You'll have a real mixture of feelings – incredible excitement, fascination, an adrenaline buzz as you realise your adventure is finally beginning, plus perhaps a bit of anxiety too. It is similar to starting a new job or going to university, just more intense. Depending on where you've travelled to and when you arrive, you may experience a real culture shock. It may be hot and humid, dark or cold. There may be terrible poverty around you and one thing is for sure, it will be very different from home.

As you adjust to your new lifestyle, the excitement of the initial situation – all those smells, sounds, sights and the general atmosphere of the surrounding country – may start to subside and things may feel tougher, especially as a bit of homesickness may kick in. By working through this and adapting to the culture, you will become more confident and able to enjoy your adventure. In the hearts and minds section in chapter seven, there is more about adapting to new cultures, which links in with culture shock. You will probably settle into the travelling lifestyle after a few days and living out of a rucksack will seem totally normal. You will meet new people and you may feel nervous about this; it's part of life, but before long you will be great friends. In hindsight, there will not be a point where you can identify when these strangers became friends.

These first few days are a rapid learning curve, particularly if this is your first major adventure abroad. Make sure you've got a clear plan for this time, even if it's just to relax for a few days to get accustomed to the new environment. If you're arriving in the morning you will have more time to check out potential accommodation, but if you're expecting to arrive late pre-booking a hotel and getting a cab is advisable. To get the most out of the area, you should supplement your background research from books and the internet with personal advice from friends at home and backpackers you meet en-route. In particular, they will be able to recommend good places to stay, things to do, reputable companies (and they can let you know the going rate for these services) – all key issues to your average backpacker.

ACCOMMODATION

During your adventures you may stay in different types of accommodation – nice hotels, not so nice hotels, apartments, backpackers' hostels and lodges, guest houses, tents, mud huts or even sleeping out under the stars. Your choice of accommodation will be influenced by budget, time of day, country and personal choice. You are unlikely to stay in top-class hotels as you backpack around, but the occasional night spent somewhere slightly nicer is very refreshing and can be money well spent. Along the same lines, if you arrive somewhere in the dark, with no idea of where to stay, you will be better served heading for somewhere that looks secure rather than going off into the back streets for a bargain hostel. When travelling in India, we had a long and interesting journey on a very basic bus. On our arrival in an unknown town in the early hours, we chose a hotel that looked safe. We certainly weren't too fussed about cost – although it only turned out to be a few quid extra anyway.

In choosing your accommodation, focus on the things that matter. A friendly place that is secure and clean is fine, particularly if your attitude is positive and you have the right kit with you. Likewise, adopting the right attitude and using the techniques in the hearts and minds section will generally make your visit more sociable; your hosts will be more likely to go the extra mile to make your stay more comfortable and fun.

If you are going on a long-term aid project the sending organisation may have a house (a loose term) that aid workers share, or you'll stay in some sort of guesthouse. It is important to check out the section on hearts and minds in chapter seven, Personal and Cultural Issues. If your 'house' is some sort of mud hut in an isolated village, don't panic – with a bit of initiative you should be able to make yourself comfortable by using your own things, supplemented with local equipment as necessary.

Some travellers choose to camp. If you're travelling where very basic accommodation or poor quality local tentage is likely to be used, take a tent or a Gore-Tex bivi bag and a nylon basha sheet as previously described on page 30. You can make an adequate tent out of a basha sheet if push comes to shove, or use it to improve an existing tent. A Gore-Tex bivi bag is great if the tent leaks, as it will keep your sleeping bag dry and you warm.

If you are relying on a Lonely Planet or Rough Guide to tell you where to stay, bear in mind that many other travellers will have read the same information, so the places they mention could be fully booked. There are generally plenty of places to stay in any town or village, as long as you arrive at a reasonable time and do some basic planning, but if none are available you'll have to move on or use your initiative – we have ended up sleeping on a Thai beach before now which was no big deal, except for the fact that the tide came in and we had to move rapidly!

FOOD

Obtaining good, safe food can be a bit of a challenge, particularly in the developing world. Where you eat usually depends on how long you are in an area. If you are travelling through a country there is more of a tendency to eat at restaurants, but if you are living and working in an area for a long period of time, as many Gap Year people will be, you may well buy and cook your own food.

Everyone has to eat, so you will find a source of food somewhere. Local towns will usually have their equivalent of supermarkets. If you are planning to stay in one place for a while, check out the food supply issues in advance if you can. Your sending organisation should be able to help you. When purchasing meat you have to be careful; try to establish how long ago the animal was killed, and think about the look and smell of the meat. When cooking eggs, to avoid bad ones, break them individually into a mug before adding them to other ingredients. This stops your breakfast or dinner being ruined by a bad egg, which smells, looks, and is disgusting.

It is a good idea to have some back-up food and snacks like dehydrated soups and dried ready meals, as well as plenty of teabags, coffee, milk powder and sugar. Don't forget to maintain hygiene standards – washing hands before preparing food, making sure tea towels and washing-up cloths are kept clean and ensuring that food is not cooked by anyone with a stomach bug.

TRANSPORT

You are likely to experience a wide variety of transportation methods – aircraft (both very big and very small), buses/coaches, taxis in their various forms, trucks, cars and four-wheel-drive vehicles, motorbikes, boats, trains, hitch-hiking, bikes, walking and possibly animals. Your journeys and your choice of transport will be sure to leave significant memories. One of my most recent is that of hurtling down a mud track at 4.30 in the morning in an old coach, while the driver spent most of his time chatting to his mate!

Then there was the time our bus was stopped by Shiite Muslims, but that's another story.

The vast majority of serious incidents and insurance claims centre around transportation accidents, so you'll have to be a bit streetwise. You cannot eliminate risk, but you can reduce it by a long way. Roads in many areas of the world have a higher risk factor than those in the UK. You need to be aware of this and also that treatment may be harder to get if there is an accident. It is also worth mentioning that you should be wary if you come across an accident, as you may be accused by passers-by of causing the accident, or it may be a set-up to rob you when you stop.

Let's look at each mode of transport to highlight potential risks:

Large aircraft – these are regulated if they fly internationally, so enjoy the journey, get a good book and relax. Internal airlines are not regulated, even if they have big jets. The country information section of the Foreign Office website should have details of any really unreliable airlines – these are rare but not unheard of.

Small aircraft – in some parts of the world small aircraft and helicopters are a common mode of transport. You may use them for leisure or to get to different locations. There is not a lot you can do in terms of safety (the majority of us are not equipped with the skills to suss out a pilot or check an aircraft); but on the bright side, it's in the pilot's interest to survive as well!

Buses/coaches – whether you are going travelling for one week or one year, you are likely to use these a lot, particularly in the developing world, where buses tend to be extremely cheap. They take every form, from completely beaten-up vehicles that were obsolete before Noah's Ark was designed, to surprisingly modern vehicles. In the developing world, vehicles are people's livelihoods and represent a vital form of communication, so there is a significant incentive to keep them running. Animals and freight of every conceivable type may find their way onto the vehicles because they are the only form of transportation – these things will make your journeys interesting! But how do you decide which is safe? How do you know if it has had good maintenance? How do you know the driver has had some sleep?

When deciding whether to use a specific bus or coach, it's best to research other travellers' experiences. Combine this with local knowledge of good or bad operators, guide books, local geography, length of journey, comfort of the vehicle, the timetable/route and, to a lesser extent, cost. Use your gut instinct – it may be that the prospect of a 48-hour journey on a battered and uncomfortable coach is inconceivable (a reasonable assessment) and that you would be better off catching a train, or even flying. In India on one occasion I chose to fly, rather than endure a miserable two-day coach journey. It cost £50 extra, but believe me the money was well spent; it got me there in two hours, feeling fresh and ready for adventure.

If you do use local buses and coaches, you are playing by local rules and you have to respect these. Timetables are not always adhered to – you could try checking their reliability with local people, other travellers or guidebooks. Make sure that you take sufficient fluids and something to eat that will not go off, such as chocolate. It can be tempting to eat food that is offered through the windows at bus stops and towns, but this may not have been freshly cooked. The effect of dodgy food can hit within minutes – it's not worth the gamble.

As for using coaches in the Western world, the long-distance journeys are in the USA and Australia. I have done both. The Australian journey was fine and good fun, mainly because the coach rarely stopped except for the odd tourist site and refreshments. The USA was different. I caught the Greyhound bus from Seattle to New York and can honestly say it was my worst coach travel experience ever. Over a four-day period the coach stopped every few hours and everyone had to get off. It was exhausting. I still remember seeing the New York skyline and feeling an enormous sense of relief that the journey was finally over. The next year I flew everywhere and probably, on balance, spent the same amount of money but felt human at the end of the journey.

Taxis and other local transport – in any foreign country there will be a local taxi service. Different countries in the developing world will use different vehicles, including pick-ups, rickshaws, minibuses, and motorised three-wheeled scooters. Vehicles such as pick-ups and minibuses regularly carry about three times their capacity and I have even seen scooters in Delhi with four people on them! Taxis are generally reasonably safe, but be clear how much you are going to pay before you start your journey. Try and pick up from others a sensible going rate – not a price that either rips you or the driver off. Be open and friendly with your drivers as they can tell you a lot about the local area in a short amount of time.

Traffic can appear completely mad in developing countries no matter what form of transport you use, though quite often it is fairly slow and accidents are fewer than you may think. Use your common sense when deciding how to travel. Sitting on the back of a very overcrowded pick-up is obviously more dangerous than sitting in a roomy cab wearing a seat belt (which is always advisable). It's easy to get side-tracked on the money issue, but you may only be paying a bit extra for using a cab. Try and have loose change for paying, particularly on local journeys. There is no point in negotiating a sensible price and then giving a very high denomination note.

If heading off on a long journey it may be sensible to hire someone to drive you – this normally means a group of you getting together and negotiating. It can be a lot of fun as the driver can use his local knowledge to point out anything interesting – treat them well and it could be like a mini tour.

Trucks – normally the only way you will travel in these is when you are on some sort of adventure tour, in which case local people or the tour operator will be driving and taking care of things. If you choose to hire or buy and drive one yourself, refer to the four-wheel drive section below. Remember to protect your eyes from grit, maintain sun protection and, if the vehicle gets stuck, make sure you don't get hurt in the extraction process.

Cars – you may wish to hire a car for a few days. This tends to apply to the developed world where vehicles are generally in good condition, particularly if hired from a well-established company. It is common practice in Australia and the USA to hire for one-way drives, particularly across their amazing deserts. You should be suitably equipped and it is vital to remember that if you break down when driving across the desert, do not leave the vehicle (refer to the next section for more details).

Four-wheel drive vehicles – if you are contemplating driving a four-wheel drive (4WD) vehicle on a long overland trip then you'll need to get advice from books, people and courses on how to drive off-road, the type of vehicle, logistics, recovery, maintenance, navigation and so on. Driving long or short distances in a 4WD requires the recognition and attainment of certain skills. It's a fun way to travel, but it can be difficult to schedule your journey as all sorts of things can happen. You may be delayed getting across a river due to flooding, trees may be blocking tracks, the tracks may be washed away, you may have to winch your vehicle out – the list goes on. This may sound challenging but it is rewarding – true character-developing stuff.

You will generally be prepared for challenges such as vehicle breakdown, but if you do get stuck in some incredibly isolated place, don't attempt to walk out, especially in desert environments. Your vehicle will give you shelter and a base, and hopefully you will have some supplies. If you are on a road someone should eventually come along who can help or give you a lift. If you feel you may go in to areas where this is not the case, you can buy emergency satellite locators. In an emergency, parts of the vehicle can be used to make distress signals: mirrors for sun reflectors and burning a tyre with some fuel to make black smoke.

Use your common sense and try to prepare for any eventuality. It may be a good idea to make sure someone knows where you are going, and although it sounds obvious, it is essential to take plenty of spare water, some spare food and your travel survival kit.

Motorbikes – in terms of long distance trips the same principles apply as for 4WD journeys. Motorcyclists should know how to maintain their bikes, and there are books available on the subject. Ensure that your first-aid knowledge and kit are comprehensive, and that you have read the wilderness first-aid section carefully.

Do not hire motorbikes abroad, as your insurance is unlikely to cover this. Too often, due to the excitement of the moment, people ride with inadequate protective clothing, with severe consequences in the event of a crash.

Boats – these range from big ferries (over which you have little control), to much smaller island-hopping boats or even dug out-canoes. In the developing world, regulations and international laws won't necessarily be enforced in the same way that they are in the developed world; however, it is in the interests of the owners to keep their boat afloat and to get everyone to their destination safely. If you do feel unhappy for any reason, don't use the boat, as alternative transportation or another boat will usually be a possibility. In the unlikely event that the worst happens and your boat sinks, your rucksack will float and it can be used as a buoyancy aid, providing the contents are packed in a waterproof liner as described in chapter three, Equipment. If you are with a group you can strap rucksacks together and thereby stay close to each other. If you have to do any of this, you will be having a very bad day!

Trains – can be really interesting and good fun. I've used them in Kenya, India, New Zealand and the USA and although they were more expensive than other forms of transport, it was well worth the extra. There is something special about them that's hard to define. My main advice in this area would be to go first class in developing world environments – it's generally not that much more expensive but have a look at second and third-class and you'll see the benefit. I have a fantastic memory of arriving at Old Delhi station at 4.30 in the morning. Monsoon rains were coming down and the steam and smoke from the trains was all around, as were hundreds (or thousands) of Indians – an incredible atmosphere.

Hitch-hiking – the popularity of this form of travel has reduced due to a few nasty incidents and because the growth in adventure travel has meant lower transportation costs. I have hitched in the USA, around New Zealand and in Kenya; plus, of course, in the UK. Hitch-hiking can get you out of tricky situations, but it can potentially get you into even trickier ones!

I would suggest you do not hitch-hike in the USA. It is difficult to know which areas are safe and which are ruled by gun law or have a major drug problem. You only have to visit Florida as a tourist to get advice about car-jacking and checking your vehicle at night. It is a real pity as the people and country as a whole are terrific. Flights and car hire in the USA are reasonably priced and provide comfortable travel, although the Greyhound coach (as described earlier) is not much fun.

While I have met some interesting people while hitch-hiking, I would not recommend it as a routine form of transport; apart from the safety issues, more reliable forms of transport are often cheap and easy. In the developing world, you may also be depriving an area of much-needed income.

In an emergency, however, you may have no other choice, and if this happens to you, bear the following tips in mind:

- If female, do not hitch-hike alone or even with another woman.
- If possible, hitch as a pair.
- Choose a sensible location – can a vehicle pull over safely and can they see you in advance?
- When a car stops, if you don't like the look of the driver, don't get in. Ask where they are going first, so you have an instant reason to politely refuse the lift.
- If it is possible, hitch a lift with a family, as this is likely to be safer.
- Look presentable and like a backpacker, but do not have valuable items such as cameras on show.
- Once in the car, take a polite interest in your hosts, and stay awake even if you're tired. This is important from a personal security point of view. If you stop, and it feels appropriate, offer to buy them a drink or meal (depending on where you are, as it could be expensive!).
- I have also accepted meals from people who have offered me lifts; there are potential risks in doing this and you will have to use your judgement.
- Maintain positive, confident body language. Stay sharp.

Bikes – there are some superb mountain bikes available. If you are intending to use this form of transport you will already have a reasonable appreciation of what you want to do and what you need. The type of bike, airline regulations for carrying the bikes, panniers and other kit, what the roads are like, your objective, the climate and physical fitness are all areas you will need to consider. It's simply a matter of researching, planning and getting the right equipment. Pay particular attention to maintaining fluid intake, and make sure you can repair your bike in the event of a significant mechanical failure.

You could hire a bike whilst away. Be aware that, especially when off-road, you can build up significant speeds with an increased probability of falling off – so cycle carefully, wear a helmet and stay in control. Mountain biking is great fun but recklessness can result in severe injuries. If you want some inspirational literature on cycle touring, read Josie Dew's books.

Walking – despite the many forms of transport available, you are still likely to do a considerable amount of walking – so make sure you have some comfortable trainers.

Animals – it is possible that you could end up on an elephant or another local animal, although they are more likely to be used for load carrying. My advice is to do what the animal owner says!

COMMUNICATION

When travelling, you'll probably want to get in touch with family and friends at home. This keeps them informed of your adventures and may stop them worrying. It can also be nice for you to get news from home. In today's world of global communications, you can keep in touch very easily, whether by phone, text messaging, e-mail or post – and make your friends at home a tad jealous! While there may be places in the world where communication is still a challenge, for most Gap Year travellers distance will be no obstacle to keeping in touch. You can also contact other backpackers, to find out information or arrange to meet up. I love receiving e-mails and letters from people I have met travelling.

On the down side, you can have too much of a good thing and spending all your time on the phone or in internet cafés may detract from the travelling experience. In the days when communications were few and far between, they were probably appreciated much more. In my view, writing letters and postcards still has a lot to be said for it, and, if you are being sponsored, a letter shows your sponsor that you have put in that little bit of extra effort to thank them. Ruth, who writes about her travels at the beginning of the book, made a conscious decision to limit her contacts with home to writing and receiving letters, as she enjoyed this more than e-mail messages. Too much contact with home can trigger homesickness.

You will have to find a system that suits you, and personal circumstances will play a large part in this. The internet makes it easier to monitor mortgages and the like while travelling, but if someone reliable is sorting out these things for you back home it allows you to concentrate more on your adventures. It is also worth mentioning that there are still many places where reliable internet access is hard to find.

Telephone. Mobile and land-line telephone systems are much more available and reliable than they were even a few years ago, and occasionally people in really bad situations have managed to summon help using text messages to family thousands of miles away (though you should not rely on being able to do this!). I have even been in relatively remote parts of Africa and managed to make a mobile phone call.

I would carry a mobile phone on a trip if I was leading a group as it would be useful from a safety point of view (assuming the battery can be periodically charged). This is, of course, in addition to other survival equipment, not in place of it. If you are buying a mobile specifically for your trip, make sure it's a tri-band one which will work in more places, and that it has a long battery life. Check with your service provider whether your phone will work in the countries you are visiting. Mobile calls from abroad are not cheap, although text messaging is a budget way of sending news.

Land-lines are good but can be expensive, particularly from hotels, so be very careful not to run up a huge bill. In many countries you can buy phone cards for use in a call box, though it is not always that simple. It is true to say that virtually every large town in the world has some form of phone system – although it can be a bit more of an effort in the more remote ones.

Satellite phones are very expensive, but can be used in places where no other communication is possible. They might be considered for larger organised trips to remote areas.

E-mail. Most Gap Year travellers will know their way around the internet and e-mail. As well as communicating with home or other backpackers, the internet can be useful for getting medical information and up to date travel advice. Make sure that you set up a reliable e-mail address before you go abroad. There are lots of free memberships available but I have found that sometimes they don't seem to work as well as the ones where you pay a monthly subscription – it may be that you get what you pay for. It might be worth setting yourself a regular time when you check your e-mail, say weekly, otherwise you may feel the need to go into every internet café you pass.

You could also consider setting up a website or blog that you update regularly, adding your thoughts and pictures for family, friends and sponsors to see.

Letters. It helps if you write legibly, which I don't! There is something special about receiving a letter, so I would encourage backpackers to send letters and postcards and also family and friends to write back. If you do not have a fixed address, the Post Restante system comes into its own – people back home simply send a letter to you c/o Post Restante at a post office in a certain town. You can then collect them using your passport for identification. Some areas are really organised, others much less so. Make sure your surname is written in capital letters to avoid confusion, as not all countries use the English system of forename and surname. You do not need to inform the post office that you are going to use this system, and they will keep letters for a reasonable length of time (weeks to months, depending on the country). There is sometimes a small charge to collect each letter.

6

MONEY AND PERSONAL SAFETY

SAFETY AND SECURITY

If your personal safety is jeopardised, it is most likely to be while someone is trying to steal your money or valuables. To safeguard yourself, and your money, I suggest you follow this advice:

Avoid looking like a rich tourist. Conduct yourself in a confident manner, but do not act in a way that makes you stand out from the crowd. If you need to walk through a potentially dangerous area, avoid walking past blind corners or any area where would-be thieves could be hiding. By removing their element of surprise, it is less likely that you will be targeted.

Don't carry a lot of cash and divide what you have between secure pockets (preferably front and zipped), your day rucksack and maybe a money belt or waist bag. Personally, I think that money belts and waist bags are over-rated, as they are easy to remove with a knife and are not very comfortable. Serious thieves can spot them a mile off, and you don't want to encourage close contact with knives. If you are confronted, give your valuables to them without a fight. Your possessions are not worth your life. Carry your day rucksack or bag under your arm, so you can keep an eye on it.

You don't need to carry all your money with you, and you could leave some in a hotel safe, but you will have to use your judgement as to how secure this is. If there isn't one available, or you are not confident that it is secure, then you can set up a decoy by leaving a small amount of money somewhere obvious, as a distraction from other money and paperwork which is hidden elsewhere. Under the pillow or mattress is one idea (as long as the hotel staff do not change the bedding daily, otherwise they may think it is a tip!).

Potentially, someone may attempt to break into your room when you are asleep. You should not get obsessed about this, but for peace of mind make or buy a doorstop. It is lightweight and small, and even if someone picks a lock a doorstop wedged on the inside will make it difficult to open the door, particularly quietly.

Make sure you have enough local currency in a wide variety of denominations, as a local market trader in a small village is not likely to have change from the equivalent of a £20 note. It also highlights the differences financially and culturally between you and them, and draws unnecessary attention to you as a rich foreigner. I remember nearly getting caught out in Bangkok when I paid a TukTuk driver with a large note due to a lack of change – my fault. He simply drove off with my money! It was broad daylight so I chased him and caught up with him at some traffic lights, 500 metres away. I shouldn't have pursued him, but I was angry and this coloured my risk assessment. I did retrieve my money, but I should have avoided the situation in the first place by having smaller change.

Keep a note of your insurance policy details and emergency phone numbers – on your person, in your bag and with a reliable friend or your parents at home – so they are always accessible. Memorise the phone number for your home contact.

MONEY MANAGEMENT

There are several ways to carry your money:

- Cash can be carried in local currency, sterling, euros or dollars – in some countries dollars are preferred to pounds sterling. In many developing countries local currency is not available until you arrive.

- Travellers' cheques are the only reasonable option if you are carrying a lot of money, as they offer good security. However, you should remember that you cannot always cash them in the back of beyond.

- Cashpoints are found in many countries, but remember that you need to have money in the account to be able to take some out. Make sure you keep enough cash on you for an emergency reserve, as cashpoint machines have a habit of running out of money when you need it most; don't be down to your last penny when you head for the machine. There are exchange rate and commission issues to consider, although the less often you change money the less often you will be charged. Finally, remember cashpoint cards can get damaged, so look after them.

- Having money transferred to you is an option, but is a real pain and with proper planning is unnecessary. In the developing world there may be issues in terms of money disappearing and administration, so it is best avoided.

- The ability to manage your bank account from thousands of miles away, via the internet, can be useful, as you can transfer money between accounts or pay credit card bills. Personally, when I'm off on my travels, I want to get away from all that stuff.

- Credit cards can be used and they will ensure you avoid carrying loads of cash; but it is easy to build up an enormous debt, as the credit card companies allow high credit limits. Okay, you're away having the time of your life and the realities of paying debts are a long way off, but the money will have to be repaid at some point. The way to have peace of mind is to work hard and save up, so that you don't have to borrow. When you get back from a trip there is usually a sense of anti-climax, and having to deal with a massive debt is very depressing.

- The black market gives an improved exchange rate, but it is a big mistake to use it. Firstly, it is illegal and you lay yourself open to the laws (and prisons) of the land, which will not be very sympathetic to you cheating their country out of foreign exchange. Secondly, your personal safety will be compromised. You can easily end up in the wrong place at the wrong time; at best you'll lose your money or at worst – who knows. Don't be greedy.

7

PERSONAL AND CULTURAL ISSUES

GETTING ON WITH PEOPLE

Backpacking adventures can produce the most amazing bonds between people that will last a lifetime, as relationships are forged, tested and strengthened by the many shared experiences of travelling. However, there is a danger that relationships will be strained, so what can you do to try and prevent problems in this area?

It stands to reason that when you are travelling with other people, either on a long or short-term basis, there will be times when you don't get on. This may be made worse by tiredness, illness or homesickness. These feelings aren't limited to travelling relationships, but don't let them get out of hand, or they can lead to real problems and unnecessary hassle.

If you are choosing a travelling companion, think carefully about who they are and how they'll react in adverse circumstances. If you are going on an adventure tour or organised Gap Year project, you will not have the option of choosing your fellow travellers. You will be expected to travel and work with people you have never met, or perhaps met briefly on a training weekend. Try not to make instant judgements in these situations. People adapt at different rates to new environments, cultures and conditions. Homesickness and mild illness can affect people differently. Some people may be well-travelled and can adapt more quickly, but those who adapt at a slower rate can, once they settle, be worth their weight in gold. Try to be sensitive to your companions; support each other and remember that everyone has bad days. If someone is troubled or a bit down, just listening to them with genuine interest, combined with the odd word of encouragement or advice, can make all the difference. The bulk of problems that I have come across centre around a lack of communication and trust, so be prepared to listen to others. By treating everyone as you would want to be treated, there is a positive atmosphere of looking after each other and watching each other's back, which is conducive to good relationships. The 'I'm all right Jack' approach is not the way to carry on. While it is important to make some time for yourself, to listen to the radio or read a book, a timely brew made for someone can make all the difference.

'SEX, DRUGS AND ROCK 'N' ROLL'

This section highlights how people's behaviour can change while travelling, so you can be prepared for the consequences. Inappropriate actions could ruin your trip and potentially mess you or someone else up for life. Everyone's behaviour changes when they are on an adventure abroad – it's all part of the experience – but you'll need to remember to think before you act.

You may have watched television programmes about holidaymakers abroad, leading you to believe that the only way you can have a good time is to drink yourself legless each night in an attempt to impress someone enough to get them into bed. As you have read this far, you will hopefully have a bit more sense and realise that you don't have to have a sex, drugs and rock 'n' roll lifestyle when away (or at home for that matter) to have a really great time.

Have some beers, dance the night away, but keep your brain engaged and make sure that it links in with your body. If you lose your money or any possessions through being incapable of looking after yourself, get injured or wake up in a bed next to someone you barely remember meeting and suddenly wonder what diseases you may have caught or whether you may have conceived a child, you only have yourself to blame. Most of the serious incidents I have had to deal with when travelling or leading trips have been alcohol-related.

In some countries, where there is a thriving sex trade, it is very easy to obtain sex. The major problem (alongside the possibility of prosecution) is the very high risk of contracting potentially devastating sexually transmitted diseases. In some Asian countries, the prostitutes and their pimps are very clever and persuasive, so I would suggest you don't follow anyone anywhere no matter what they offer. Remember that HIV is everywhere, and is especially prevalent in red light districts in the developing world. Don't forget other diseases – Hepatitis B, for example, is 100 times more infectious than HIV, and Chlamydia may lead to infertility and other very serious gynaecological problems at a young age. You have been warned.

The only sure way of avoiding infection is abstinence or staying with a faithful disease-free partner. If you have any doubt on your partner's sexual history you should use a condom, but remember this is only safer sex – not completely safe. If the weather is too hot or cold, condoms may be damaged. Condoms bought in the developing world may look the same but may not be reliable, and sizes vary. The commonly used anti-malarial doxycycline can inhibit the action of the oral contraceptive pill, as can an upset stomach.

'Smoked some dope in Asia. Lost three days.' Traveller, 2001

Sadly the drug culture around the world is now more rife than ever, the UK being just one sad example of the spread of this cancer. Depending on where you are going, the exposure you can get to a variety of drugs is considerable. When I was hitch-hiking across America in the mid 1980s, I was offered various drugs on about 70% of the rides. Avoiding getting involved meant a combination of diplomacy, politeness and firmness.

Even back then when I gave talks on my adventures, I gave out an anti-drugs message, remarking on how a lot of those offering drugs looked completely spaced out and sick. You may wonder why I even got into vehicles with people like this! It centres around waiting in the middle of nowhere for hours and hours, and not always realising how stoned the occupants were due to a hefty dose of naivety on my part.

The fact is that drugs mess you up, and cost you money; money that ends up in the pockets of criminals. There is no such thing as dabbling in drugs and most addicts started by simply experimenting with their mates. Drug addiction, like disease, is no respecter of age, sex, race, background or money. Don't let the freedom of your travelling adventures start you on this road – maintain self-discipline and strength of character and just say 'no'.

The quality of the various illegal drugs varies. Think of it this way – would you take an aspirin or any other prescribed drug if you were unsure of its manufactured quality or dosage? I suspect not, and yet this is exactly what people are doing when they use illegal drugs.

Once under the influence of drugs you are making yourself much more open to thieves, and other dangers such as violent assault or having an accident due to an inability to think straight. It is the start of the road to addiction, which is not a pretty sight, and can cause absolute heartbreak in families.

There are other considerations too. In many countries the penalties for carrying or using drugs are mind-blowingly severe and the attitudes are, quite rightly, uncompromising. The jails in developing countries can be horrific, as some high profile cases have demonstrated.

In summary:

- Do not use or buy drugs. You do not need them in order to have a fun, fulfilling and enjoyable experience, wherever you may be.

- Do not carry any package given to you by a person you do not know. It could contain anything, and its contents are almost certainly illegal.
- Do not become so blind drunk that you do not think clearly and carry out actions you later regret.

The above information is not meant to constrain you in any way; indeed, as I hope you now realise, the opposite is true. It's actually about making sure you have a great time and come back remembering it all, in good health and ready for more.

As for "Rock and Roll", I have seen some great local live bands when travelling – there seems to be far more of them in places like Australia, New Zealand and the USA compared to back here in the UK. We need to catch up!

HEARTS AND MINDS

Wherever you go in life and whatever you do, you need to adapt to the people and places you encounter. This process is obviously much more pronounced when you travel, as you are heading off to very different cultures.

It is important that you behave appropriately and respect the people and countries you go to. If you show respect, it will be reciprocated; the local people will help you and welcome you into their culture. You should appreciate that it is a real privilege to be accepted by a community, and that those who follow in your footsteps will benefit from your positive legacy.

Apart from behaving in an agreeable manner, there are other ways you can help to promote this mutual respect:

Research where you are going, to find out if there are any culturally specific interpretations of behaviour, such as how hand gestures and dress code are perceived. Religious issues need to be understood, such as needing to take off your shoes if you go into a temple or someone's house.

Try to learn some basics of the language, preferably before you go or very quickly after arrival. Local people really appreciate you trying to speak their language. Make an ongoing effort to learn the local language, particularly if you are going to be in an area for a long time. You will probably be able to fall back on English in a lot of countries where it is a national language and even in other countries many people will speak a smattering of English. Other European languages such as French (in parts of West Africa) and Spanish (in Central and South America) may be the national language, and it should be easy to find somewhere to learn these before you leave.

Maintain an open, positive body language – open palms and eye contact are great. Body language says a lot; don't be arrogant, you are the guest in their village or country, and the local people will recognise a condescending attitude very quickly. See Sarah's account below for an illustration of cultural differences about the importance of time-keeping.

Be careful that homesickness does not taint your feelings towards the local people. It can cause you to have a negative attitude to the country you are visiting which can, not surprisingly, be interpreted in a negative fashion by your hosts. Understand that these feelings are only temporary, so try not to act on them and hang in there – it'll be worth the wait!

If you are going to be staying for a long time, I'd advise getting involved in all areas of daily life. Don't just sit there and expect people to do everything for you – load the Land-Rover with them, or offer to collect water or fire wood. Talk to your hosts, play football or volleyball with them (football is an international language on its own), or watch the local school team playing sport.

Do not run away from the culture, either physically or psychologically – get in there and get involved.

If your visit is long term, you may feel it is appropriate to give gifts (such as bargain watches or pens) to enhance relationships. I am not a great fan of this, and particularly not of giving money, as it's attitudes and actions that should count. While you can't buy your way into people's hearts, using small gifts in a limited fashion can get you brownie points very quickly. Be careful about how it is interpreted, as you don't want to be seen as a permanent source of goodies – it can actually hinder your relationships and it is not necessarily beneficial to the local community. It can also set a precedent for others who follow and this could create problems. It is best to give gifts only to those people you know well.

You may be asked to provide medical care if your trip is to a country in the developing world, especially if they think you have a medical background. The military have used medical care to win the hearts and minds of the local populace for many years but it is different in this context. Offering the odd plaster or bandage is fine if you have enough (and take plenty if you anticipate being asked for them) but that should be it. Saying no can be tough, but if medical aid is not properly thought out it could interfere with work and training that is being done elsewhere in the region, and give unrealistic expectations to the local people. However, if someone you have got to know is really ill, what you do is up to you and you will probably not want to distance yourself. If you are going with an organisation, ask them their views and experience.

If you are going abroad to work, particularly in the developing world, accept that their style of leadership and working will probably be different from yours. It may not be wrong – work with it. Don't always accept the first job you are offered if you feel it's not appropriate, but try to suggest an alternative. Try not to offend, use your common sense, be positive and humble and, if necessary, be politely firm.

Capturing the moment – photography. It's perfectly natural that you will want to get photographs of the people you meet and the places you visit. If photographs are taken in the proper manner, you can get loads of great photos of pretty much everything you want, without offending anyone – so you can re-live your adventures and inspire (or bore) your friends and relatives afterwards!

When photographing local people, it is important to take account of their feelings. How would you feel if someone kept sticking a camera in front of you while you were going about your daily life? Bear in mind the following advice:

Make sure your camera kit is not openly displayed – it identifies you as a rich Western tourist with a lot of expensive equipment, marking you out as a target for thieves. I carry my camera kit around in a small rucksack or keep it tucked out of sight inside my jacket. I get it out after I have sussed out the picture I want to take, snap the shot, then put it away fairly quickly. Many people carry a compact camera attached to their belt, in the zipped case that they are sold with. This is perfectly reasonable in most situations, but get a dark-coloured case so it is less conspicuous. If you are in a small community for a length of time, the local people will get used to you having a camera, so it may be all right in this situation to wander around with one.

You should ask for permission before you take photos of local people. If you don't speak the language, smile, point to your camera and use friendly, obvious signs and they should understand. Use local greetings and acknowledgements, and if they say no, be gracious. In some areas they may ask for money, especially if you are on well-trodden backpacker routes – this will be made obvious. Sometimes it's a matter of principle for them as well as an additional income.

By behaving in a relaxed and polite manner, you are more likely to persuade your subject to pose – the key is not to be too pushy. When photographing someone, a short zoom lens will produce a good portrait, but consider using a wide angle lens, getting fairly close and composing the picture with the person slightly to one side and their environment behind. I have managed to obtain some powerful shots like this. By having an open, friendly attitude and showing common courtesy (such as opening doors for patients), I was able to photograph traumatic events in a Ugandan medical clinic. This was very rewarding, as the resulting shots helped raise money for my aid organisation.

Sarah spent three months teaching English in Peru. Here are some of her thoughts on adapting to a different culture:

> *When I was preparing for my trip to Peru, my primary concern was with the language barrier. I had been listening to tapes for months but had never had any formal lessons or much of a chance to practise the language. I hadn't given much thought to the cultural differences I was about to experience, apart from the typical 'what will the food be like?'. I was much more preoccupied about how I was going to teach English to a group of people when I couldn't even speak their language! As it turns out, the language seemed to take care of itself, with a little help from a phrase book. The main preoccupation in the first month or so was with the different culture. It's very difficult to see why people would have different values to those we hold in our Western culture. The main example, which I still have difficulty getting my head around, is time-keeping. This probably wasn't helped by the fact that my father was a military man. Time-keeping and punctuality are emphasised a lot in the military! So you can imagine the shock of finding myself in an environment where people just didn't seem to worry about this. It was not because they were being rude, or selfish, it just simply isn't important in their culture. I became used to adult students*

wandering into my evening classes up to an hour late, without any sign of apology. It did not occur to them that I would find this very rude, and I found it hard not to take this as an insult to my teaching! The fact is that people did not expect to know exactly when something was happening, apart from morning, afternoon, or evening. We used to turn up at the bus station for a 3 o'clock bus and the driver would not be there until 5 o'clock. In the UK, people would be up in arms about this. But no-one seemed to be bothered; they were quite happy to sit and wait indefinitely, something we are not very good at in our Western culture! In the afternoons, shops would close for siesta time. We spent quite a few weeks trying to work out what time they closed and when they reopened. We eventually realised closing time was whenever the owner was feeling a little sleepy, and opening time was when he decided to get up from his siesta! We learned to tolerate this and not to expect anything to happen on time, but I never quite managed to understand how anything got done in Peru! The most important lesson that I learned from my stay was to be open-minded, and not to try and understand but just to accept that I was a tourist in their country and if that is how they do it, then fair enough! Actually, they all seemed a lot more contented and much less stressed-out than a lot of people I see in the UK.

8

MANAGING YOUR TIME – WORK OR PLAY

You've managed to get yourself abroad for your adventure – but what are you going to do? It's a good idea to be clear about your objectives and decide what you are going to do when you get to a given area. This doesn't necessarily need to be detailed but, unless you know why you are going there, it could be a waste of money. Checking guide books when you arrive is a bit late.

The general premise for your trip will dictate what activities you do and when you do them. You may have planned to spend a considerable amount of time in one area and look for work there. If you end up doing a pretty boring job, make the most of it, work hard and be reliable – this helps future travellers. By being conscientious you may also be able to create opportunities for more rewarding work. It is important you work legally, and most countries will have a realistic set-up for this. Don't try and cheat the system as it has a habit of catching up with you. Once you have found a job and somewhere to live, it's like living in any new town, and you can sort out how to manage your time between work and play.

If you are on a formalised Gap Year project you will have specific work to do in a given time frame of weeks or months. Depending on the organisation you are with, you may have time allocated for travelling during or after the period of work. If not, you may just decide to head off after your work finishes. Once you have been in the country for a while you will learn from other people, the locals and the sending organisation about the interesting places to see and how to get to them. This will complement your own research.

If you are on an adventure tour of some sort, you will normally have a defined itinerary, potentially with some flexibility to add to or to amend the planned activities. Again, it may be possible to travel independently at the end of the group trip.

You may choose to travel and not to work at all, with the aim of relaxing and exploring. I usually funded such trips through working extra shifts in operating theatres before I left. It may be easier and more lucrative (especially taking exchange rates into account) to work an extra month or so in the UK than it would be to work abroad.

CHOOSING YOUR ACTIVITIES

Being a tourist. With so many guide books around, you can't fail to find out about a place and what there is to see – hitting the major tourist sights will be easy to do and will be good fun.

Down at the beach. You could head for the beach and a day of swimming, snorkelling and sunbathing, followed by a terrific dinner of freshly caught fish at a fraction of the UK price. Whilst travelling in Thailand, my wife and I did this – it was a tough way to spend the day, as I'm sure you can imagine! You may find a lot of beautiful, isolated beaches on your travels, but do consider water safety issues. There are not usually problems, but ask for advice; an area may be known for having bad tides or other hidden dangers. I feel the need to say this having seen a Japanese tourist pulled from the sea in Sydney and given mouth-to-mouth resuscitation.

The sea is a living entity – so watch out for things that bite or sting. It's very unlikely that you'll be bitten 'Jaws-style' by a shark, but being stung by a jellyfish can be quite severe. Along certain stretches of the Australian coast, there are box jellyfish which can administer a fatal sting. Take note of local warnings and be aware of potential hazards.

Scuba diving. If you are a qualified scuba diver, then you will know about areas that are good for diving, and the necessary safety regulations. You may, however, plan to learn to scuba dive or do a 'try dive' while abroad. The undersea world is awesome and you do not have to go very deep to see stunning sights. I've seen a large Angel shark ten yards off the coast of one of the Canary Islands, in only four metres of water. All diving schools should be PADI registered – if you come across one that isn't, give it a miss. These days you can do 'try dives'. These take various forms, but basically you go down 3-5 metres on a one-to-one or one-to-two ratio with an instructor, after having been schooled in SCUBA techniques beforehand (usually in a swimming pool). What I would suggest, if you think this interests you, is to contact your local sub-aqua club (BSAC in the UK), as they normally do 'try dives' in swimming pools. This will give you a feel for it, help you to see if you like it and ultimately should enhance the experience of diving in the sea. I qualified as a diver many years ago, but all I do now are 'try dives' when I get to an area with good diving. Ruth, our eldest daughter did this when she was eleven years old off the coast of France – she loved it and there were no problems, apart from her dad being a bit stressed!

Canoeing. I have had some excellent canoeing adventures – running two-week trips in Canada, paddling the Delaware and other rivers when teaching at summer camps on the eastern side of America and travelling in tiny, flimsy canoes to some small but very attractive backwaters in India. A recent canoeing adventure in south-west Uganda was also memorable when I paddled out on Lake Bunyoni in a dug-out canoe with Ruth (a GapYear traveller who writes about some of her adventures at the beginning of the book). We were heading to a restaurant to meet some friends but, on reaching the middle of the lake, I asked Ruth which direction we should go. Her reply was, "I don't know, I thought you knew!" It proved difficult to get directions, as there was a distinct lack of passers-by; but, suffice to say, we found it in the end.

Canoeing is relatively easy to pick up, and fairly safe in still waters, but you should ensure you have a lifejacket and know the basics. Don't copy my example above – know where you are going and any hazards you might face en route. It is sensible to travel with other canoes if you are going any distance from immediate land-based help. Canoeing at sea or in fast-moving water is a very different matter in terms of the risks, and should only be undertaken if you have the appropriate training, equipment and back-up, which is beyond the scope of a general book like this.

White-water rafting. Your travels may well take you to areas where you'll have an opportunity to go white-water rafting, through some mind-blowing rapids and scenery. If you're after an adrenaline rush, this one is for you. It's really good fun and comparatively speaking it is good value. Tourist rafting routes are generally pretty safe (it's in the interests of the company to make it so), but you'll need to use your common sense and follow the safety procedures given in the pre-trip briefing. Some companies have kayakers who accompany the trip and marshal at key points, although this depends on the severity of the route. Make sure that your lifejacket is done up correctly, that you are wearing a helmet, and that you have appropriate footwear that will not fall off.

If the route has big rapids, you could be thrown overboard. If you don't panic, you should be fine until you find a safe place to come ashore. As you go downstream, face downstream, so that you can see where you are going. You MUST keep your feet up, preferably sticking out of the water, and your legs slightly bent so you can push off obstructions. Do NOT put them down until you are in an area where you can see the bottom and you can stand safely, otherwise they may get stuck between boulders or in the roots of a tree or other obstruction. The current will then force you under the water and it may well be impossible to resurface.

Bungee jumping and other aerial pursuits. These may be on your agenda; although, personally speaking, leaping from a bridge with a bit of elastic tied to my feet or jumping out of a perfectly serviceable aircraft has never appealed to me! If you're after a thrill, the adrenaline will be in plentiful supply. Most places which offer bungee jumping are regulated and very careful (they would go out of business pretty sharpish if they got it wrong), but no activity is risk-free, so use your common sense. The same things apply to other aerial activities, such as parascending and hang-gliding. These sports are generally pretty expensive, but if you enjoy airborne challenges you might as well take advantage of the opportunities.

Chris grasped every opportunity to try his hand at extreme sports in the year before he started drama school:

> *Whilst in my post A-level gap year travels I learnt to scuba dive, bungee- jumped off a bridge, went on a 4x4 off-road safari, sailed on a 70-foot racing yacht, white-water rafted and sky-dived. Snow-capped mountains, majestic lakes, crystal-clear air, ancient canyons, beautiful rivers and streams and thousands of miles of rugged countryside ... as far as I was concerned the only way to truly appreciate these marvels of New Zealand was either upside down hanging from a length of industrial elastic, or from 12,000 feet readying myself to jump out of an aeroplane.*

> *I chose to 'Fly the Pipeline' – a 102-metre bungee jump in Queenstown, New Zealand's capital of extreme sports. The bungee platform was on a single-span suspension bridge built on the site of an 1864 gold-sluicing water pipeline above Shotover River. On the way to the platform in a Land-Rover, the driver gave a commentary on the history of gold-mining in the area, in an attempt to take my mind off the fact that I was about to jump off a bridge! I enjoyed about 4 seconds of freefall before being shot back up and inevitably back down again. Eventually, I was lowered into a jet boat for a high-speed trip to the bank before making my way back*

to the platform, where there was the opportunity to repeat the action. There are many bungee jump companies all over New Zealand, each offering different deals with extras such as photos and videos, so it is a good idea to shop around.

I went on a scuba-diving course at Koa Toa in Thailand, which offered a huge range of scuba diving and snorkelling opportunities. I completed my PADI open-water course for about 7500 baht, which at the time was roughly £110. This included accommodation, tuition and equipment hire. The company provided a beach barbecue every night (not included in the price) and many group evening activities. Videos and photos were also available.

The sky-dive I did in Taupo, New Zealand (which was cheaper than Queenstown) was the most exhilarating of all the extreme sports I participated in whilst travelling. I got kitted out with a jump suit, hat, gloves and goggles. After watching a five-minute instruction video, I was loaded on to a plane, taken up to 12,000 feet and, along with an expert parachute partner, told to jump. For the 45 seconds of freefall, you do nothing but enjoy it.... and scream ... lots! Then the 'chute opened and I had five minutes of gentle gliding to view Taupo from a very unique angle.

WILD COUNTRY ADVENTURES

To get the most out of wild country experiences in mountains, jungles or deserts, you'll need to have certain skills and knowledge, whether you are organising the trip yourself, going with an organised tour or doing a bit of both. In this section I will outline some general principles; then, in the next chapter, I shall discuss survival in mountain, jungle and desert environments in more detail.

Firstly, research where you are going, preferably in-depth before your departure. There are plenty of guidebooks around and loads of information is available on the internet, but you will also need some good maps as they provide an added dimension and really bring an area to life. If you can't read maps, learn before you go – if you can read a street plan of your local town or draw a map from your house to the local pub, then you already have some basic knowledge. Thereafter, it's just a case of getting a local Ordnance Survey map and practising. Maps abroad will not be exactly the same, but the principles are identical.

Ask around to get ideas and to find the best operators. Some years ago I met up with some friends in Washington State, USA, to backpack through the Cascade Mountains. As we were limited for time, I asked a forest ranger for ideas and he gave some terrific advice on where to go. We had a superb adventure backpacking through some incredibly isolated and spectacular mountains, and still talk about it today – we would not have had such a great experience without that local knowledge.

Researching the area will enable you to evaluate the proposed itinerary and to check whether a proposed adventure tour company knows what they are talking about. It ensures you find out the relevant facts, so they do not turn into problems.

Some general questions you need to consider are:

- What are the logistics of going to a given area, in terms of accommodation, transport and food?
- What will the weather be like?
- How much will the temperature vary between day and night?
- Are there any security issues (personal or political)?
- Will the trip involve high altitude?

Adventure tour operators

These are companies (a loose term in some places!) which you can hire to organise a trip for you, but as you're preparing for a challenging adventure you'll need to be sure exactly what the tour operator will provide. When I climbed Mt Kenya I simply hired a guide for the final ascent, but at the other end of the spectrum you can join an organised truck safari for six months. Decide how much support you'll need, and which of the available operators will provide what you want, before deciding who to hire. Recommendations from fellow travellers who have used the operator themselves are useful, but do your own research too, as you may want something different from the people you've spoken to. Key questions are:

- Do they seem like a reliable company?
- Do you have confidence in the leaders?
- What is the itinerary?
- What will be the highlights?
- What equipment do they provide, and is it well maintained?
- What's included in the cost, and does this represent value for money in your opinion?

The answers to these questions will leave you better prepared for your trip, such as highlighting the need for you to bring equipment. I decided to take my own tent on a trip with a small trekking company in India, based on my research which suggested that the tents provided would not be of high quality. This turned out to be a very wise move indeed, as I like staying dry!

It is sensible to use local people or agencies in some form or another, because they have knowledge of the area and contacts, both of which may be invaluable. In addition, you are supporting the local economy and meeting local people will give you a better feel for the culture. I have been on a number of trips with local people in Africa, Nepal and India. Each was organised in a different way and required a varying amount of input from the traveller, but all were excellent, as I went with a positive mindset – remember the advice from the Hearts and Minds section.

It is worth highlighting that some operators may not have an extensive medical kit or experienced first-aider, so make sure your travel survival kit is up to scratch. Dr Hugh Matthews, The Outdoor Experience medical officer (who describes his adventures on a trans-Africa six-month trip at the beginning of the book) went on one of these trips when he left school and ended up dealing with a lot of medical problems instead of the trip leader. This was on the basis of his first aid training and experience that he gained on an excellent half-day's course run by Royal Army Medical Corps Combat Medical Technicians, on one of my hospital personal development programmes.

Organising your own wild country trip

These can be much more of a challenge than going with a tour operator, and if you are thinking of doing this you should have the appropriate skills and experience. Make sure you have the necessary equipment, including tentage, food, medical kit and other items, depending on your mode of travel. The logistics of your trip will need careful attention, such as sourcing food supplies and fuel for your stoves. Allow for a period of acclimatisation and get to know the local people and culture. You may be used to doing everything yourself, but in developing countries it can be more practical to hire people to assist you.

Wild country adventures, whether organised by yourself or someone else, will require survival skills to some extent, and often involve certain types of adverse environment, which present their own problems. The next chapter goes into more details about these, and following this is a section on wilderness first-aid. If your travels are going to take you off the tourist trail, then this information is for you.

9

SURVIVING IN ADVERSE ENVIRONMENTS

EMERGENCY SURVIVAL SKILLS

We all get ourselves into situations we would rather not be in. Many nasty situations are predictable and with a bit of planning they can be avoided, but accidents and unforeseen incidents do happen, no matter what you do – how you deal with them can stop matters from getting worse. If something does happen to you, the key is to have a positive mental attitude, initiative, the ability to think laterally and to carry some very basic kit with you to help make things easier.

If you are unlucky enough to find yourself stranded, employ damage limitation – your first priority should be to find shelter before adverse weather sets in, or night falls. Look at someone living on the streets in any big city and you will see that this is the first thing they sort out – they protect themselves from the elements. Your shelter will depend on where you are and on the environment. It could just mean paying for a better hotel if this is the only, or safest, option. However, hotels may be few and far between on wild country adventures. You may be able to use a bus shelter, a bridge, dense forest, a cave or barn, but potentially you might have to make a shelter from materials that you have or can find. Having a penknife and a few bits and pieces on you, such as nylon cord and a polythene survival bag, can make a world of difference in this situation. Don't forget that good waterproof clothing is a form of shelter too, and by having it on you should be able to keep yourself dry. In a wild country situation, there is a very real danger of hypothermia. When sleeping rough you need insulation under you as well as around you.

Water, food and fire come next. We all have to drink and eat, and it pays to have a spare bar of chocolate or two tucked in your rucksack in case you are caught out, but in the short term food is less important than water. Water is essential and you may need to ration what you have or source it from streams, which is why you need water purification tablets in your travel survival kit. If the situation and resources permit, you may want to build a fire; this gives heat and light and is psychologically reassuring. If you can find a can or something similar, you can also heat up water or food on it. The matches and candle in your travel survival kit can be used with paper, cotton wool, dry grass or small pieces of wood to make a fire. If you are planning a wild country adventure, a block of solid fuel from a military stove is an excellent way to light a fire. It is not necessary to build an excessively large fire, and you should remember to collect all of your firewood while you have good visibility, as you could get hurt hunting for firewood in the dark.

Thereafter, survival is all about positive mental attitude and good decision making. If it's simply a case of sheltering for a night prior to catching the next bus, that's no big deal; but in more extreme situations things can be more serious. Judgements may have to be made, such as whether to stay or move. If you are lost, find a place on the map where you definitely knew where you were. Calculate how far, given your mode of transport, you could have travelled from this point, eliminate places you definitely are not at and you may be able to work out where you are now. If the weather is really foul and you have shelter and water, it's best to sit things out until they settle.

Bronco Lane, who writes on jungle survival in this book, survived a night on Everest in an emergency shelter at 28000ft in a snowstorm. He lost some fingers and toes, but made it back alive. I have had the privilege of listening to Bronco lecture on his Everest adventures, and he describes vividly how he and his climbing partner Brummie Stokes attribute their survival to the sheer will to live and to mutual support.

MOUNTAINS

I have had some amazing times exploring mountains in different parts of the world, some fantastic adventures shared with great people in many varied terrains and cultures. As I sit here and write this, memories of just a few adventures come flooding back – sunrise on Mount Kenya with Andy; a snow storm on a Himalayan Pass with Sarah; Boys' Own stuff in Washington State with Paul and Derrick, when winter storms hit early; exploring the Norwegian Arctic wilderness with Hugh, and encountering black bears with Dave trekking on the Appalachian trail and in the Adirondacks.

By doing adequate preparation and research and sticking to the principles outlined in the equipment section in terms of staying warm, dry and comfortable, you will also enjoy your mountain adventure. You'll need to take sensible clothing and footwear, some spare dry clothes for use in your tent or hut in the evening, a warm sleeping bag, a compass and a map of where you are going (make sure you know how to use it). It's a good move to get fit before you go, as mountain adventures tend to be physically challenging. Try to have a realistic view of what can be achieved, appreciating all that a successful trip entails.

There are some important medical conditions that you should be aware of if you are going into the mountains – hypothermia, altitude sickness and frostnip/bite. It is also possible (although much less common) to overheat from exertion, so read the section on heat illness under 'Deserts' as well.

Hypothermia. Your normal body temperature is 37°C. If it drops to 35°C, then hypothermia will have started. It is caused when the body's ability to generate and conserve heat is overcome by heat loss. If you are properly clothed, dry, well-fed and fit, then it should not occur; so, again, it's down to using the old grey cells.

The wind chill factor is important here, as an ambient temperature of 0°C with a 12 mph wind is the equivalent of –10°C on the skin.

Normally, hypothermia develops insidiously over a number of hours. There are various symptoms at different temperatures. Initial visible symptoms include unnatural behaviour for the person – a quiet person may be loud or a loud person quieter – walking much faster or slower than normal, looking cold, pale skin, blue lips and shivering. In some respects it may appear that they are drunk and they may deny there is any problem at all. Once a casualty's temperature really starts to drop (to the 31-34°C range), things are grim, with loss of consciousness and the risk of cardiac arrest at the lower end of the scale. At the higher end of this range the casualty may try to remove clothing as they become very confused.

Treatment, at any stage, is to stop and get immediate shelter, checking that the others in the group are all okay and that they put on extra layers of clothes due to the cessation of exercise. Any damp clothing should be removed, the casualty wrapped in dry clothing (with particular attention to the head) and put in a sleeping bag with an insulating mat underneath. The air should be warmed with a stove if possible. If the casualty can take warm drinks and food these should be given, but make sure they are conscious enough to do so, otherwise choking will result. If another person can get into the sleeping bag, it can help to warm up the casualty. Do NOT under any circumstances give alcohol as this can kill by dilating blood vessels in the skin and causing blood to shoot away from the core of the body.

If the casualty is unconscious, move them extremely carefully as in a very hypothermic person there is a significant risk of cardiac arrest. Finally, should, through some bizarre set of circumstances, a hot bath be made available, do not put a severely hypothermic casualty in it, as this can also cause cardiac arrest.

In many years of exploring mountains all over the world and running many trips in awful weather, I have never had a case of hypothermia – it is, on the whole, preventable.

If trekking with a daypack (as is commonly the situation where you have guides or porters), it's not a bad idea to carry a survival bag. These are made of orange heavy-duty polythene and can easily fit one person plus sleeping bag inside them. They weigh next to nothing, and are compact when folded. Leave them unopened at the bottom of your pack, as they are a nightmare to refold once air gets trapped in them. They provide instant protection from the elements and can also be cut open to provide a large polythene sheet with which to make an emergency shelter.

High-altitude sickness. A lot of research gets done on this subject – partly because you can head off to some exciting country and climb mountains, all in the name of science! Despite all this, the way to deal with altitude sickness is extremely simple and as usual prevention is better than cure. It catches a lot of people out, as high mountains are not limited to obvious places such as the Himalayas – Africa has some seriously high mountains, as does the USA, Europe and South America.

There are three types of mountain sickness; namely, acute mountain sickness (AMS), high-altitude pulmonary oedema (HAPE) and high-altitude cerebral oedema (HACE). AMS will almost always precede HAPE and HACE and the distinction between all three can be blurred. All are caused by less oxygen getting to your tissues, due to the reduced air pressure and reduced oxygen in the air. Do keep it in perspective – hundreds of thousands of people go to high-altitude areas each year and very few have a major problem. Just follow the advice outlined below and you shouldn't either.

Recommendations on how to acclimatise vary but in general, above 3000 metres, each night should be spent no more than 300 metres above the last, with a rest day every two or three days. Should a stay of more than 300 metres above the last be unavoidable, then a rest day should be inserted to make it an average of 300 metres a day. Some authors suggest 600 metres of ascent over a two-day period, which may on occasions be more practical. Some people may find this slow, but altitude sickness is no respecter of age, sex, fitness or experience. In fact, it has been argued that physical fitness can encourage altitude sickness, as it's easier to ascend more quickly if you are fit. When considering trekking companies whose journeys involve high altitude, check their policy on acclimatisation. There is a vogue to consider taking medication to help you acclimatise. I am against this. All drugs have side effects and they offer false security. There is no substitute for acclimatising at the correct rate.

The worst case of altitude sickness I have experienced was in Denver. High-altitude sickness was never discussed in those days, and being fit from a summer's adventures I was advised by a family on the plane that Longs Peak was a good mountain to climb at 4580 metres. It seemed like a lot of fun, so I duly made my way to the mountain and backpacked up to my campsite at 3300 metres with a full load of tent, food and so on. The following morning I set off at 5am and hiked to the top. By the time I got there I felt the altitude, which is not surprising as I had been at sea level 24 hours previously. By the time I got back to my tent I felt pretty ill with a thumping headache. I descended rapidly, but continued to suffer from a high-altitude cough for several weeks. In hindsight, I did it all wrong and I was somewhat fortunate – subsequently, I have acclimatised much more sensibly, and so should you!

Acute mountain sickness. This is the most common form of mountain sickness. If you ascend rapidly to an altitude of 2500 metres you will feel breathless, which normally settles but can lead on to AMS. The symptoms normally start six to twelve hours after arrival at high altitude, although it may be as long as one or two days. Normally, it will precede HAPE and HACE. Features include:

- Headache - the most common symptom; worse during the night and morning and on bending over
- Loss of appetite, nausea and vomiting
- Dizziness, sleep disturbance and weakness
- You may feel and act like you have a hangover and will often be irritable and want to be left alone

Providing you do not ascend any more, the symptoms normally last for 24 to 48 hours, so if there is any suspicion of AMS you should stop. If there is no improvement, the symptoms worsen, or there are any features of more severe altitude sickness, then you should descend. Someone with these symptoms should be watched by another person who is not affected. It is fine to take normal painkillers for the headache.

High-altitude pulmonary oedema (HAPE) is serious and results from an accumulation of fluid in the lungs. It is made worse by cold, exercise and dehydration. The victim will have a fast breathing rate (more than 30 times a minute in severe cases) and a vastly reduced exercise tolerance. They are likely to awaken from sleep with extreme difficulty in breathing, and be unable to catch their breath on rest. As it gets worse, a dry cough may develop with blood-stained sputum. Their skin and lips may start to turn a dusky blue colour. As in other forms of mountain sickness, the first and most effective form of treatment is to descend to below the point where the symptoms first started. This should be done as a matter of extreme urgency. Oxygen will produce immediate results and can be life saving if it can be sourced. There should be minimal exertion of the casualty and they should be kept warm and in the upright position.

High-altitude cerebral oedema (HACE) is rarer than HAPE and again is extremely serious. It is caused by the brain swelling, due to lack of oxygen. The border between this and severe AMS is blurred. It has been described at altitudes as low as 2500 metres, but is more likely to occur above 3500 metres.

Symptoms include confusion, disorientation, irrational behaviour, clumsiness, hallucinations and ataxia (poor co-ordination, similar to being drunk). This can be tested for by drawing a straight line 8 feet long and getting the casualty to walk heel to toe along it. Using the arms for balance is normal, but if the person falls off the line or has major difficulty, the test is abnormal and you seriously need to consider descending as soon as possible. An unaffected member of the team can be used as a control. The progression from initial symptoms to coma may be as little as 12 hours. Hypothermia must be excluded, as the symptoms are similar.

Like HAPE, anyone suffering from HACE must descend immediately, no matter what the time of day or night, or they are likely to die, though you should think about the safety of the group when doing this. Oxygen should be given if available. It is possible that the casualty will go into a coma, in which case you have a very significant problem in terms of evacuation and management of the casualty. This is discussed in the Wilderness First-Aid section.

Sleeping. Sleep patterns do change at altitude. Sleep may become irregular and some individuals may wake up breathless. This can start at 2500m, but is more common over 4500m. A period of deep breaths may be followed by a period of lack of breathing, which can wake the sleeping person up with a feeling of suffocation, and it alarms companions. It does not appear to be related to high-altitude sickness.

Existing at high altitude is no big deal, despite the above. Ascend at a sensible rate (as previously described), maintain a good fluid intake, have an awareness of the symptoms of high-altitude sickness and be prepared to adjust your programme accordingly.

Frostbite and frostnip

These cold-weather injuries are unlikely to be an issue for your average Gap Year adventurer. However, they are included because you just never know where you may end up!

Frostnip. If trekking, the most likely extremity problem (although it's still unlikely) is frost nip. The areas we are concerned with are the fingers, toes or nose. They will become waxy white, numb and very cold. As usual, prevention is the key, using adequate dry mittens and footwear, as well as keeping your whole body warm, dry, well-watered and fed. The treatment is to re-warm with body heat. It is painful as the blood returns. Don't massage the area, as underlying tissue damage can result. If you are concerned about your fingers or toes, stop and check, as frostnip can turn into frostbite within a few hours. If it really is that cold you should maintain an awareness of the danger and also look out for facial frostnip.

Frostbite. In some mountaineering books you will see horrific pictures of frostbite, which is much more serious than frostnip. The whole or part of a digit, hand or foot becomes numb, white and frozen. What you need to do then is to get to a medical facility as soon as possible. While it's possible to move on a frozen foot, this should be avoided if possible, and you should not attempt to put weight on a thawed limb.

When practical, the treatment for feet is to remove the boot and sock and dress the foot loosely with padding and bandages, making sure you put individual dressings around the toes. You should administer painkillers and antibiotics if you have them. Re-warming or thawing is extremely painful. The same procedure applies to fingers. Put a loose dressing separately around each finger, after placing some sort of (preferably sterile) gauze around the digit. The hand should be bandaged in a mug-holding position, using a bandage in the palm of the hand as something to hold on to.

As frost-bitten limbs thaw they can look revolting, with large blisters forming (and bursting) and black skin. Long-term results can be very good, but treatment can take months.

THE JUNGLE

My good friend Bronco Lane has spent a considerable amount of time travelling and working in inhospitable jungle environments. Below, he offers advice based on his extensive experience:

The primary jungle environment means one where the tree canopy covers the whole landscape, stopping any of the sun's rays from reaching the forest floor. Given the profuse growth of vegetation due to the warmth and high moisture levels, visibility is reduced to a few metres (twenty would be the norm). Therefore, slow movement on foot and accurate navigation are the major considerations, combined with the high humidity, which produces a huge loss of body fluids.

Before going to the jungle, I would strongly suggest you find a thickly wooded area and practise cross-country movement off-track for a few days, in pairs or more. Concentrate on accurate navigation and developing a 'sixth sense' when you become mis-placed. The compass very rarely lets you down.

It would not be unusual for even the most acclimatised individual to need fifteen pints of water per day whilst walking in jungle with a small load. Sourcing a suitable replenishment point of clean drinking water means either extensive use of purification, or finding small, flowing and sandy-bottomed streams, which do not flow through any habitation upstream of you.

Maps of jungle areas are normally based on air photography and, because of their inaccessibility, are rarely checked on the ground. Therefore, the detail will probably be less than accurate, in particular for tracks or small features and rivers.

Foot movement off-track will be painfully slow and exhausting, as you encounter the forest dead-fall (dead vegetation which has fallen to the ground) and thick undergrowth. Available tracks do offer a more acceptable method of getting to your destination, although most will not be marked on maps, as only the locals use them. So, if a track is going in your required direction, make use of it. An accurate use of your compass and time/distance are the prime considerations, as would be the hire of a local guide.

Rivers are obviously a major obstacle and suitable bridges will be non-existent. A small river can quickly become a raging torrent following a rainstorm. It would be unwise to make an overnight stop near any river, keeping above it by at least 7 metres. However, river banks do offer a natural highway of sorts and if followed for long enough, they will always get you to habitation (or the sea). Animal tracks invariably will follow a river bank, or a ridge line. Remember though that most animals do not need the same height clearance as humans, so they may be impassable to you. Movement through swamps should be avoided at all cost.

Having thrashed your way through the jungle for a very tiring day, a safe, restful night-spot is essential. The prime considerations for its selection must be environmental danger from flooding and also dead-fall from the trees above. It follows that a small ridge line, away from water, where the canopy is minimal, should be sought. The main intruders to a good night's sleep will be mosquitoes and ants.

A mosquito net, insect repellent and a hammock or pole bed under a waterproof shelter sheet gives the best rest possible, as it keeps you off the jungle floor and away from its myriad inhabitants.

Due to the high humidity and rainfall your clothes will invariably be wet. To enjoy a good night's rest, changing into a dry sleeping suit and socks is highly advisable. However, the next morning a high degree of personal discipline is required to change back into your still wet clothes! Clothing should be loose fitting and lightweight. Long trousers are a must, tucked into your vibram-soled ankle boots. The shirt will need long sleeves, worn rolled down to protect you from vines, insects, etc., hooking into your flesh.

Cuts and scratches quickly become septic in the high humidity, as do leech and tick bites. Another daily occurrence will be sores produced from a loaded rucksack rubbing against wet, sweaty hips and shoulders. To enjoy travel in jungle areas requires lots of self-discipline, perseverance and positive team-work, combined with a slowly, slowly approach as you learn the ropes.

In addition to your water-proofed map and compass, essential items of personal gear will always include: rucksack, small machete in sheath and belt, candle, lighter, matches, pen knife, shelter sheet, hammock, mosquito net, light-weight sleeping bag, water bottles, water sterilising kit, spare change of clothes (kept dry), spare cord, head torch, dehydrated rations, mess tin and spoon, mug, small stove and fuel, medical kit.

Bronco stresses how wet the jungle is, so refer to chapter three, Equipment for advice on how to keep your kit dry. If it's a demanding situation you're after and you are fully prepared to be tested, exploring the jungle is an opportunity for you to conquer a challenging environment. Do take heed of Bronco's advice, as it is not an environment for the faint-hearted; significant challenges, both mental and physical, are guaranteed on a jungle adventure.

DESERTS

Deserts can be blisteringly hot or very cold – the word desert simply means lack of rain – and they are incredibly wild places. One of the most spectacular sights I have ever seen was when I was in Kenya. There was tremendously wild and rough terrain all around us until we went over a small rise and we suddenly saw an enormous turquoise lake stretching to the horizon – Lake Turkana, the Jade Sea.

On this trip it was extremely hot and the common sense things we did are the basics for desert survival – consume plenty of fluids, wear a sun hat and sunglasses and use lots of suntan cream (and in my case lip cream as my lips dry quickly).

If you are planning a trip by yourself or with friends, maybe backpacking for a few days or driving across the desert, you will need to think carefully about what you are doing. Deserts are spectacular in their raw, rugged beauty, but they can be very unforgiving. If backpacking, keep the load light and however you are travelling, prepare and plan carefully. In some desert areas it is mandatory to notify the local police of your intended route, and even when that is not the case, it is worth informing someone at your destination of your expected arrival time, so that help can be summoned if you do not get there.

As dryness defines the desert, one of your major concerns will be water. Always carry plenty, including enough in reserve to prevent heat illness, and make sure you know where you can re-supply. Ensure your water bottles are strong, so that you don't lose valuable water through your water bottles leaking.

Remember that even hot deserts can be cold at night, so as part of your research check what the temperature range is and plan accordingly.

Heat illness. Heat illness takes two forms – heat exhaustion and heat stroke. Heat exhaustion is the mildest form and is caused by a lack of fluids combined with excessive sweating and/or activity in a hot environment – which could be the high mountains, not just the desert, tropics or jungle. Heat stroke is much more serious, a life-threatening emergency, and is caused in the same way. The dividing line between heat exhaustion and heat stroke is not particularly well defined.

Heat exhaustion can manifest itself over several days, as the body gets out of balance in terms of hydration. The symptoms are varied and can include headache, dizziness, sweating (but not always), chills, fatigue, irritability, anxiety, nausea and vomiting. The heart and breathing rate may also speed up and the temperature may be elevated – quite a varied list. People can be more predisposed to it if they have had some sort of stomach bug.

It is fairly straightforward to deal with heat exhaustion, and you should expect a rapid improvement following treatment. If you suspect someone is suffering from it, stop what you are doing and if possible get them into some shade. They will need 1 to 2 litres of watery fluids over a 2 to 4 hour period (these can be very lightly salted: say a small pinch per litre). If you can, pour water over their head or body to aid cooling. The casualty should then rest and drink regularly for the next 24 hours. If you have a thermometer and the casualty's temperature is 39°C or above, they should be treated as a heat stroke victim.

Heat stroke is much more serious and is a medical emergency. The body will have completely lost its ability to control its temperature, the casualty will have ceased to sweat and will become extremely unco-operative prior to losing consciousness. Their skin may be dry and hot but this does not always apply. Treatment is to cool the person as quickly as possible, giving fluids by mouth if they can take them. Lots of cold water, wet towels or clothing should be placed on them and you should fan them to aid cooling. It is essential to monitor and maintain the airway if they become unconscious. Evacuation to a medical centre is a priority as there may be significant internal damage. It's best to assume that any fit person who becomes unconscious after exercise has heat stroke, and you should follow the advice given above.

Heat stroke is rare, but mild exhaustion is much more common, and may often be put down to a simple faint. The basic measures to prevent heat illness are:

- Recognise that there is a danger of heat exhaustion.
- Maintain adequate hydration levels. This is a really important point and as a rule of thumb I try and drink at least 25% more than I feel like.
- Drink before you start your physical activity.
- Don't dress too warmly. If you are hiking, accept being a bit chilly when you start, otherwise you'll have to stop to remove layers of clothes.
- Be prepared to change your schedule if someone has heat exhaustion.
- Wear a sun hat. I soak my bush hat in water to help keep me cool.
- A useful tip is to freeze water or fruit drink in half-full water bottles the night before a trip, then fill up the rest of the bottle the following morning. The frozen liquid will gradually defrost during the day and encourage people to drink, because the fluids are ice cold and refreshing. This facility does not always

exist, but if it does you will be very popular! I always did this when leading groups in hot weather in the USA.

Finally, it is worth noting that we all react differently to hot and cold weather. You will know if, like me, you dehydrate easily and need to pay attention to your fluid levels when exercising.

10

WILDERNESS FIRST-AID

This section is quite detailed and if you need to utilise some of what is covered, it would be a demanding and serious situation. However, if you are going to be isolated, you should read this section as it could save a life.

I have always liked the following quote, in that it sums up the way you have to approach this subject – use your initiative.

"I'm making this up as I go (along)"
Indiana Jones and the Raiders of the Lost Ark

Basically, that's exactly what you end up doing in a wilderness first-aid situation: making up a plan as you go along, based on what's happening at that time, your knowledge, equipment and other resources.

I will explore wilderness first-aid in two parts. I'll start with the routine stuff and the minor ailments that you might have to deal with, because it is likely that this is the worst that will happen to you. Then I am going to go through the urgent, potentially life-or limb-threatening situations. These are thankfully very, very rare, but you should be prepared for them.

The concept of being prepared is a recurrent theme in this book, so if you are going to be a long way from help it is a smart move to go on a first-aid course prior to your trip. Whilst medical aid in isolated environments (even if it's only a few hours from help) is much more than basic first-aid, it will give you more confidence and a fuller understanding of what I have written below.

MINOR AILMENTS

Bites, stings and rashes. Despite all precautions, you are likely to experience minor bites or irritation from local midges or vegetation. If this happens, you can use cream or antihistamines to treat the symptoms, and you should take advice from a pharmacist about which to take with you. It's hard not to, but avoid scratching any bites as it may cause them to get infected. When I was camping near the Golden Gate Bridge in San Francisco, I got my legs covered in a very itchy rash from poison ivy. It was a mistake I made only once! A local pharmacist recommended an appropriate lotion, which to my relief rapidly eased the horrendous itching.

Cuts and blisters. If you have some sort of cut, give it a good clean with uncontaminated soapy water and put a plaster or dressing on it. When it comes to blisters, try not to get them! If you feel a hotspot as you are walking, stop and try to sort it out. Your sock may have rucked up or your laces might need adjusting. Otherwise, stick a plaster over the spot. If you do get uncomfortable blisters, you can lance the edge with a needle (that has been heated in a flame to clean it) to get rid of the fluid inside. Keep the skin over it intact to prevent infection and put a dressing over the hole.

Colds, flu and ear infections. You can get these anywhere – treat them as you would at home by taking painkillers such as paracetamol and avoiding over-exertion. If you get an ear infection, avoid swimming or SCUBA diving until it has settled.

Burns. These range from minor to extremely serious. As they are normally minor, I have included them here. First-aid principles for all burns are the same – remove the source of heat, cool the area rapidly with water, and remove any clothing that may retain heat.

Minor burns just hurt and cause a reddening of the skin. Cool with cold water and that will be that. More serious burns are very painful and normally occur because of prolonged contact with the source of heat, with subsequent blistering. If these are small, they will usually heal in a couple of weeks, but watch for any scarring or skin contractions over joints, and seek medical help if this occurs. Burns affecting a larger area of the body, and in particular those on the hands or face, should be referred for medical attention, as should those caused by high-voltage electricity.

Nasty, full thickness burns are not always painful, as nerve endings are destroyed, although at the edges there can be severe pain. The skin looks waxy, often with charring and tissue destruction, and any deep burn can be potentially serious, so you'll need to get the casualty to a hospital. A good first-aid technique, once they are cooled, is to use cling film around the wound to keep it clean and to stop fluid escaping. If a significant burn is painless, you should worry, as this means it is deep.

I once worked in the operating theatres of a burns unit, and I remember how unnecessary a lot of the injuries were. Boiling water, stoves and cooking in general (particularly if camping) cause the majority of cases in travellers, so take care. It is far better to avoid burns than have to deal with them.

Fainting. Fainting can result from a multitude of situations - a reaction to a stomach bug or flu, too much alcohol, low blood sugar, standing too long in the heat or some sort of shock. It's caused by a temporary loss of blood flow to the brain and usually the person concerned will feel light headed before they faint, so they may even sit themselves down. If someone feels faint, get them to sit or lie down and, depending on their level of consciousness stick their head between their legs when sitting or alternatively raise their legs; both of these are pretty effective. If they are unconscious, monitor their airway, breathing and circulation carefully.

MORE SERIOUS MEDICAL CONDITIONS

This section is pretty detailed, but it will furnish you with some knowledge that will significantly improve the care you can give an injured person, particularly when combined with a first-aid course.

Basic overview

In any emergency situation, no matter where it is, there is one golden rule that you must start with: secure (make safe) the environment before you start concentrating on the areas below. This applies equally in minor and major situations, as the discipline of having a protocol to work to will give you the confidence to manage any given problem.

The basic decision-making protocol that follows is based on standard medical procedures, with a few additions to take into account the isolated environment. The protocol is divided into two: the primary survey and then the secondary survey.

Primary survey

A. Approach (or assess). Is the environment safe for you, your colleagues and the casualty?
A. Airway. Is there air coming out of the casualty's mouth?
B. Breathing. Is their chest moving, and is this moving air in and out of their mouth?
C. Circulation. Is the heart beating? Is there any sign of haemorrhage (bleeding)?

This check-list is not a one-off. You must constantly monitor the casualty and keep revisiting these points, as they form the basic framework for saving life in an emergency. Without them life will cease to exist.

Secondary survey

D. Disability. Do they have a neurological problem? In other words, what is their level of consciousness and are there signs of damage to the spine or nerves?

E. Exposure / evacuation. In hospital medicine, it is at this point the casualty may be stripped to check for other injuries. However, this can make the casualty very cold (hypothermic) in the wilderness situation, even in warm climates, so you have to check for other injuries without stripping them off. Hypothermia is serious and must be avoided. We also have to add **evacuation,** as you are going to have to work out where to take a sick person and how to look after them en-route.

So, having given you an overview, this is the detail:

Approach (or assess)

- If dealing with a road traffic accident (a major cause of injury abroad or at home), you must place a warning to stop other traffic hitting the affected vehicles, turn off the engine and put on the handbrake. If you smell petrol, get everyone clear and ascertain how many casualties there are. Remain vigilant to the danger from other vehicles when you are looking after someone – you do not want to get wiped out by a lorry as it belts round a corner because you had not stopped the traffic. Keep an eye out for broken glass as well. If there is a lot of blood around, make sure you put on some protective gloves. If you don't have any, try to improvise protection using a plastic bag.

- Make sure there is no danger from falling rocks, avalanches, animals or even people. Note what I have said in chapter five in the transport section about the potential dangers to your personal safety in the developing world, should you arrive at the scene of a road accident.

- When dealing with water accidents be very careful indeed. A significant number of deaths through drowning are those of the rescuers trying to help the person in trouble. Avoid going into the water if at all possible; use ropes, flotation devices, branches or anything else, rather than putting yourself at risk.

- Make sure that the other people you are with are okay. Standing around can make people cold and also psychologically they may go into shock and faint. Not everyone can cope in these situations – try to give them something useful to do. If you are naturally taking charge, these situations require firm, calm leadership. You will have to make rapid decisions based on what you think is right at the time – you can't do any more than that, and you can change your plan as the situation evolves. Incidents like this, whether at home or abroad, are frightening, but you have to remain focused as your actions can save lives.

- Communicate with the casualties. Depending on what has happened, they may be scared or disorientated. You need to reassure them and instil confidence, as this reduces adrenaline output, which reduces pulse rate and bleeding. Do not alarm casualties by letting them hear discussions about what you're going to do next.

I remember slipping into unconsciousness in a hotel in Wales when I contracted meningitis. I can still remember the complete authority and professionalism of the doctor and paramedics, just before I lost consciousness. They were an incredible comfort, giving a real sense of being in control, which is really important in an emergency (and also, it must be said, if you are in a leadership role in any context). You may think you cannot handle this type of situation because you are not a trained health-care professional, but actually you can; you've shown the initiative and commonsense to get yourself sorted on an adventure abroad and therefore you should have it in you to sort out the problem. Indeed, the reality is that, should you be in the highly unlikely and unfortunate position where you have to sort out an emergency situation, you will have to deliver as, unfortunately, you won't have any choice.

Airway and Breathing

Checking the airway comes first, but in reality these are linked. If the casualty is not breathing they will be dead in a few minutes, so this section is very important, and it is not always as straightforward as first-aid books would have you believe.

The only way to tell if someone is breathing is to hear or feel air coming out of their mouth while their chest is moving at the same time.

It is possible for the chest to move without any air moving in and out of the mouth, if there is an obstructed airway. The abdomen may also move up and down in this situation. So it's **look, listen, feel** – look for rhythmical chest movement, listen and feel for air leaving the mouth.

It may be easier for you to assess and monitor a casualty if they are lying flat, but the recovery position (see colour photo page 96) maintains an open airway by allowing blood and vomit to drain out. In deciding whether to move an unconscious person, you will need to balance the risk of damage to the spinal cord (which is an issue if significant force has been involved in the injury) with the risk of choking if they are not moved.

With regard to the airway and breathing, you need to consider the following:

- If the casualty is breathing and there is no blood coming from the mouth, leave them as they are and watch them like a hawk, constantly monitoring their airway, breathing and circulation. Check the rest of them as described below and make them as safe, warm and comfortable as you can, while you work out what to do next.

- If there is a rasping sound coming from their mouth (a bit like snoring) and the chest is barely moving, they have started to get an obstructed airway. Their abdomen may also start rising up and down at the same time as their chest movement is reduced. This is because the tongue, which is attached to the bottom of the lower jaw, has relaxed and is blocking the back of the mouth. This may be because they have become more deeply unconscious, and is one of the reasons why you should continue to monitor any unconscious casualty. If you have any doubt whatsoever about the casualty's airway and breathing you **must put them in the recovery position immediately.** If they have received an injury that involves force, be extremely careful as to how you move them and try to support their limbs with padding or clothing. Bear in mind, though, that your **priority at all times is the airway** and that you must always be checking for signs of air coming out of the mouth, through listening and feeling for air movement with simultaneous chest movement. More on moving the casualty can be found in the evacuation section further on in this chapter.

If there is blood or vomit coming out of the mouth and they are unconscious, then they are going to choke and die, so you will need to put them in the recovery position immediately and scoop out any blood or vomit (remember to wear gloves). Someone who is completely drunk, bordering on unconscious, comes into this category. If they are on their back and they vomit in their sleep there is a significant risk they will die, as their ability to maintain their airway is often very compromised. There is a lot of fluid and food in their stomach and if it comes up it will go into their lungs and cause them to choke. Sadly this happens every year to a small number of individuals.

Therefore if someone is this inebriated they must be put in the recovery position and ideally you should watch them even if it's all night.

I have had to do this a few times. Once, when camping in the Australian bush on a short overnight trip into Kakadu National Park, a 16 year old had, unbeknown to the group, been drinking wine very heavily all evening and could not take it due to his age and size. We put him into the recovery position after he suddenly collapsed at the table and had to clear his airway on numerous occasions as he vomited a considerable amount of his stomach contents for an hour or so. Myself, Sarah and a fellow traveller then took turns at looking after him into the small hours.

- If there is no attempt at breathing you should try to open their airway as described above. Hopefully that will do the trick and they will take an enormous breath as they work to expel the build-up of carbon dioxide. If not, you are into Cardio-Pulmonary Resuscitation (CPR) territory.

- It is advisable to go on a first-aid course, so that you are capable of carrying out CPR if the situation requires it.

- If you have to leave an unconscious person, either because you need to get help or because there is more than one casualty to deal with, they **must be left in the recovery position.** Make sure you keep coming back to check them.

- If someone has received a severe blow to the chest and is finding it painful to breathe, together with shortness of breath, they will need to be checked by a medic to look for complications arising from fractured ribs.

If you want to learn more about airway management, chat to a health-care professional with relevant experience or an experienced first-aider.

Circulation

Circulation involves two areas: bleeding and the heart beating.

The basic principal to stop serious bleeding is to apply direct pressure. Whilst wearing gloves, you should press on the bleeding point, preferably with a pad such as a field or ambulance dressing which can be tied around the injury to maintain pressure. If this is not available, use a towel, shirt or something similar. If blood comes through the dressing, put another one on top; do not remove those in-situ as blood clots will be disrupted. Head wounds bleed a lot due to the large volume of blood supplied to the head, but sufficient direct pressure will stop this type of bleeding.

It is highly unlikely but if you cannot stop the bleeding from an injured limb, no matter what you do, a tourniquet is your only option. The procedure is as follows:

1. If you can see the casualty's life ebbing away due to a significant bleed, such as from a severed artery (pulsating high volume) or a large open wound, quickly wrap a belt or equivalent around undamaged tissue higher up the limb.
2. Pull the belt extremely tight. You may need to put a stick or tent peg between the skin and belt, and rotate it to twist and tighten the belt further, to compress the blood vessels.
3. You now have some time. Get some padding and bandages and apply them tightly to the wound, while monitoring airway, breathing and circulation. After about twenty minutes, release the tourniquet. Bleeding will occur but should soon stop. If it doesn't you'll have to reapply the tourniquet and try again. Never leave a person with a tourniquet on, and never leave a tourniquet on for more than an hour.

If the casualty's heart is not beating, you will have to do CPR. You will need to learn this on a first-aid course.

Finally, a word about internal bleeding. If someone has had a significant blow to the abdomen or chest, does not feel well and has a fast pulse rate whilst resting (in excess of 100 beats per minute), you should have them checked at a medical facility for suspected internal bleeding. Additional symptoms are dizziness, sweating and an increased breathing rate.

Having carried out the airway, breathing and circulation assessments (and remember, you have to keep checking them), we now need to consider disability, exposure and evacuation.

Disability

This centres on the function of the nervous system – the brain and spinal cord. The brain is enclosed in a rigid case (the skull) and any expansion such as bleeding can be rapidly fatal. The spine has its weakest link at the neck, where it can be damaged with a severe blow or twist. The rest of the spine can also be damaged, but is better protected by muscles and ligaments.

Head injuries. This can be a really difficult area to deal with. You may ask yourself: "Has that bump on the head from playing football or tumbling off a mountain bike simply left my friend with a minor headache and that's it, or does he have a brain haemorrhage and will fall asleep tonight and not wake up?"

The other fact to note here is the similarity of symptoms from serious head injuries to high-altitude sickness, meningitis and other medical problems that involve the brain, as they are all related to increased pressure inside the skull.

The following are pointers that you can use to decide if someone needs emergency medical treatment after a significant blow to the head:

- Do they have a worsening headache?
- Do they have trouble walking in a straight line?
- Is their vision affected?
- Are they vomiting?
- Is there a significant loss of memory for events either before or after the incident?
- Are they drowsy and irritable? Is their personality different? Are they disorientated and confused?
- Have they been unconscious for more than 30 seconds (as opposed to being a bit dazed) or failed to make an immediate recovery?
- Is there clear fluid coming from the nose or any blood or fluid coming from the ears? These may be signs of a fractured skull.
- Are the pupils of the eyes different sizes?

If the answer to any of the above is 'yes', then begin urgent evacuation to a medical establishment.

If the casualty is unconscious you have a significant problem. There is a straightforward way of measuring the level of consciousness, based on the letters AVPU. These stand for:

- **A. Alert.** This means they are conscious and you do not have a problem at this stage.
- **V. Verbal.** This means that they are not "with it", but do respond when you talk to them.
- **P. Pain.** This means they don't respond to verbal commands but if you pinch their ear or rub the chest bone, they respond.
- **U. Unresponsive.** This means none of the above happens.

If a casualty is anything but alert, evacuate them immediately.

If the casualty has a convulsion, leave them until the fit has finished, making sure they can't hurt themselves on anything. You don't need to put anything in their mouth. Afterwards, check their airway, breathing and circulation.

The spine. If a neck or back injury is suspected, following a blow to the head or a nasty fall, and the casualty is complaining of pain or numbness in their arms or legs, or lacks the ability to move them, you need to immobilise and evacuate them. If someone has had a blow to the head that is sufficiently severe to warrant hospital investigation, you should treat the neck as if it has been injured.

The nerve supply in the neck is vital for breathing, so you are in deep trouble if it gets damaged. Be very careful to avoid any unnecessary movement of the neck. It is not recommended to tip the head back or twist it if someone has a suspected neck injury, although you may need to move the neck with care to keep the airway open when you put them in the recovery position – the airway takes priority. See the evacuation section later on in this chapter, where moving casualties is discussed.

Immobilising the neck can be a bit of a challenge and depends on where you are and what has happened. If the patient is lying down, then boots, rolled-up clothing or blankets can be placed either side of the head and strapped down to keep the neck still. If the patient has to walk, you could make a collar. To do this, cut a piece of insulated sleeping mat to the size of the neck, wrap it around the neck and tape or tie it in place with a bandage. Trim it so it fits well. This is very effective and will help to protect against further damage.

If the casualty is complaining of back pain with numbness in, or difficulty moving, their legs, it may indicate spinal trauma. Immobilise the neck and keep the spine as stable and straight as possible, reducing movement as much as you can. Give painkillers and, depending on the circumstances, either evacuate them or wait for rescue. Support the casualty by giving them continuous reassurance.

Exposure and Evacuation

Exposure has two meanings. From an adventure point of view, people think of exposure with regard to hypothermia. In hospital medicine exposure means that once you have followed the ABCD protocol, you need to check the casualty thoroughly for other injuries and you therefore "expose" the entire patient. This way you won't aggravate an injury such as a broken bone through not knowing about it. Don't forget to check the casualty's back for injuries as this is often forgotten. Look and feel for the following:

- Pain on gentle touch
- Deformity
- Soft tissue damage
- Fluid, which may come from an open injury

It is also important to know if a casualty is complaining of symptoms in an area where none of these is present – think about what may be causing the symptoms.

You should not strip a casualty to check for injuries, as they may become hypothermic very quickly. They should be checked with sensitivity, as privately as possible and preferably by someone of the same sex, ensuring at all times that they know what is happening (Explain to them what you are doing, even if they are unconscious). Having run many outdoor search and rescue exercises over the years, it has been amazing to see how cold people get when they are lying still in mild weather and well wrapped up, acting as casualties – and they have nothing wrong with them. Occasionally casualties will be too hot, so also be aware of this – ask them.

Key injuries to look for are limb fractures, sprains or dislocations and open wounds.

Fractures / sprains / dislocations. I have grouped these together, as it is sometimes hard to tell the difference. Generally, you will be able to identify a fracture unless it involves a small bone in the hand or foot. A very bad sprain (where the ligaments holding a joint together get torn) can also mimic a break, and although it heals more quickly it is painful and incapacitating.

The signs of a fracture are:

- **Loss of function.** This means you can't use it, e.g. you can't put weight on a leg.
- **Pain.**
- **Deformity.** Compare one limb with another.
- **Swelling.** Compare one side with the other.
- **Bruising.**

These five signs vary in intensity, so at times it may be difficult to be certain that there is a fracture. When dealing with any injured limb, it is important to check for feeling and circulation in the fingers or toes of that limb. If these are numb or white, the injury may have compromised the blood or nerve supply and the casualty will need urgent hospital treatment.

The basic treatment for an injured limb is immobilisation, prior to getting the casualty to hospital. You should move a broken arm very gently across the chest, preferably so that the hand is by the opposing shoulder. It can then be strapped in place with a sling, either a triangular bandage or by pulling the bottom of the casualty's shirt up and attaching it to the top of the shirt with a safety pin, wrapping the arm up in it in the process.

If a leg is injured, the normal procedure is to move the unaffected leg next to the affected one and to bandage the two together, putting pads between pressure points such as ankles and knees (this also works for fingers and toes on a smaller scale). If both legs are broken, it's still best to strap them together if possible. When moving legs, pull gently but firmly on them. You can also make a splint out of insulating sleeping mats, trekking poles, ski sticks, wood and many other things you might find, but make sure they are padded. Loosen or remove boots and shoes as they can restrict circulation.

Sprains can be really bad – if you tear all the outer ligaments of the ankle you could be as incapacitated as someone with a fracture (which is why I advocate boots for trekking). For minor sprains, such as a fall onto a wrist or a minor ankle twist, firmly strap the limb and keep it elevated when it is not in use. If you develop a persistent pain at the base of your thumb following a fall, you should get it X-rayed when you can, as it is sometimes a sign of a hidden fracture.

If bone is sticking out or is visible, it is called an open fracture, and you should refer to the open wounds advice below before immobilising as described above.

Dislocations tend to be of the shoulder or knee cap. Occasionally, they go straight back in, but they are often very painful and need to be treated in the same way as a fracture.

Open wounds. Remember to wear protective gloves when dealing with these. If there is a large open wound, you'll need to stop any serious bleeding using the techniques already described. If the wound is visibly dirty, then it is appropriate to clean it – especially if you are more than four hours from a hospital. You should wash it, preferably with warm water that has been boiled and allowed to cool. A pinch of salt in the water will do no harm. Putting water into a polythene bag with the corner cut off and squirting it into the wound is a good idea, as the pressure will help to remove dirt. Inspect the wound carefully, using a torch if necessary, and if there are bits of dirt or loose dead tissue, pick them out with the tweezers on your Swiss Army knife.

The dressing will depend on the size and position of the wound, but the aim is to stop further bleeding and to protect it from further contamination. A sterile ambulance dressing is often ideal. Immobilise the limb as necessary. If the injury is severe enough, you could use antibiotics if you have them. You are now in a position to evacuate your casualty to hospital.

Snake bites. Snakes will avoid you if you avoid them, so bites are very, very infrequent; but as they produce open wounds I decided to put this section here. If someone is bitten there are lots of old wives' tales about what to do, but the important things are to dress the wound, immobilise the limb completely (as if it were a fracture) and then evacuate rapidly to a medical establishment. If the snake is dead, place it in a bag and take it with you (wear gloves: even a severed snake head can inject venom). If it is cornered, remain absolutely still until it has slithered away, and try to remember its markings for identification purposes. There are not many poisonous snakes and those that are may not have injected any venom, so stay calm and reassure the casualty.

Evacuation. If you have a problem that requires evacuation to a medical establishment, you are likely to have to sort it out yourself. The degree of urgency and difficulty will depend on the problem. For instance if it's a broken arm, you can feed yourself and with pain relief you can walk until you can hire a taxi or equivalent to get you to hospital. The other end of the spectrum may involve using all your resources to stretcher a seriously injured person to professional help.

If you need to turn or lift a seriously injured casualty, whether or not they are unconscious, use as many people as you have available. One person manages the head and neck, another the shoulders, another the abdomen, another the pelvis and ideally another the legs. The person managing the head is in charge and must make it absolutely clear which way to turn the casualty and when. The shoulder person should pull down on the shoulders and the head person should gently pull on the head, maintaining a central alignment. This reduces the risk of exacerbating any potential spinal injury. You may not have enough people to manage each part of the body, in which case you will have to do the best you can, with a particular focus on the neck and pelvis. Any head supports, such as a rolled-up jacket, should be ready. Be very careful of damaged limbs. As you turn the casualty, it's a good opportunity to feel the back of their body for any injuries or bleeding. Remember, you don't need to strip them – place your hands underneath clothing in a sensitive manner as appropriate. You should communicate clearly to the casualty at all times, while checking for deformity, pain, obvious wounds and fluid such as blood. Having assessed the casualty, make them comfortable. Depending on the injury this may include:

- Laying them on an insulating mat, which protects against lumps and bumps as well as insulating them from the cold.
- Making or borrowing a pillow.
- Protecting them from the elements using a tent, groundsheet, blanket or plastic sheet – anything to keep the wind, rain and sun off. If their clothes are wet, change them.
- Giving them extra clothing or a sleeping bag if they are cold.

Having made the casualty as comfortable as possible, you will need to figure out where and how to take them for further treatment. It may be possible to contact their insurance company who will be able to advise you. If so, take local advice as well, so that you can check the insurers' suggestions are practical – for instance, a road may be impassable.

It is impossible for me to predict and offer specific advice on every conceivable problem, but my aim is for you to have a prepared mindset, so you are able to respond effectively to whatever situation you encounter. Before heading off to a remote area, find out about local medical facilities. Fortunately, most people will try to help an injured person, and there will normally be some means of transport out of anywhere that is accessible by road. If you can, and the situation warrants it, send a runner in front to make the necessary contacts and preparations for the arrival of the casualty.

Moving someone who is hurt can be a challenge. If they can walk (or limp) you will need to support and encourage them, and make sure you have enough supplies with you to survive – particularly for protection against the elements. If they can't walk, you'll have to improvise a stretcher or get some other form of help. A stretcher, for example, could be made from rope or by threading waterproof jackets with branches or poles, or by using a flat piece of wood such as a door with rope handles added on. Bronco Lane, whose jungle survival section occurs earlier in this book, has had a pretty exciting life and has successfully evacuated people using ladders and gates. If you are insured or have enough money, and they exist, you can call the rescue services. In some areas this may get you helicopter rescue, but do not expect this – a casualty may end up on horseback or even on a Sherpa's back. It is unlikely, but if you do find yourself in such a situation, you will have to figure out a solution, even if it means leaving the casualty and going for help, or sending off someone else and waiting for help to arrive – if you do send someone to get help write down on a piece of paper your location and full details of what has happened, the casualties condition and so on.

Nursing issues

There are three main areas here – confidentiality and dignity; fluid and food intake and output; and record keeping.

Confidentiality and dignity. Throughout the management of a medical situation you may need to ask personal questions and do personal things to the casualty. At an appropriate time, you should stress to them that what they tell you will not be discussed with anyone who does not need to know. It is very important that you maintain this dignity and discipline throughout, and remain focused on sorting out the situation.

Fluid and food intake and output. If you are in an isolated location and you have to deal with an incident that requires professional medical support, the casualty may require water, food or toilet facilities before reaching a medical establishment. Supplying food will contradict the normal first-aid rule of not feeding the casualty, but there is no clear-cut way of handling this. The following guidelines will help you in your decision-making process:

- If your casualty only has broken bones, fluids are the priority, though snacks can be given. Water, oral re-hydration fluids, soft drinks or weak tea are all fine. Allow them to choose from whatever fluids are available, as it will make them feel more positive. Broken bones will bleed internally – the body compensates for this loss, and taking fluids will help the body to adjust. It's best to give a small amount of fluid at frequent intervals.

- If the casualty has some sort of internal injury or is being sick, things are trickier. Stick to water or oral rehydration solution, giving little and often.

- If they have diarrhoea, it is important to maintain clear fluid intake to avoid dehydration.

Now for the next – not so pleasant – bit. We all need to go to the toilet and this includes casualties. Just remember the last time you wanted to urinate but had to wait. Painful, wasn't it? Because the subject is embarrassing, the casualty will probably wait until their bladder is at full capacity before mentioning it, so they are likely to be very uncomfortable. The same applies to defecation. If you are calm and thinking clearly, you should be able to use your initiative to get through this whilst retaining the casualty's dignity – it's all part of caring for an injured person. Here's a bit of guidance:

- If someone is ill and needs the toilet, they will be more concerned with achieving the end result than feeling embarrassed. I speak from experience! When I was recovering from meningitis, the after-effects meant I could not move without the help of two nurses and my drip stand for me to hold onto. I could barely lift my arms initially and was suffering from bad diarrhoea (a side effect of the antibiotics). I will leave the rest to your imagination but suffice to say embarrassment was the last thing on my mind!

- If you can walk or carry the person to a toilet or bush, that is clearly best. You should be prepared for being asked to hold them, undress them or even clean them. Be calm and act as if you don't mind this. If you think it would ease any tension, you could joke about it.

- If possible, try to get same-sex helpers. If not, at least try to keep the patient covered to maintain their dignity. Remember, however, that this is a medical emergency situation, so the casualty should understand that above all else, it is their safety and cleanliness (not their modesty) that is paramount.

- If they are unable to move, it may be feasible for them to urinate into a water bottle or other container. I was impressed by the initiative of a doctor I know who converted an oxygen mask into a funnel to help relieve a casualty on a high-altitude mountaineering trip.

- If they are immobile and need to defecate, then things aren't necessarily impossible. I read of one account where a mess tin was used as a bed pan; or you could use cling film, a bowl or a polythene bag. All this is highly unpleasant stuff, but it is very, very unlikely to happen. If it does, just do the best you can.

- Wear gloves!

Record keeping. This is important (as if you haven't had enough to do!). A written record of what has happened and what you have done is really useful to health-care professionals. You would be amazed at how a seemingly insignificant bit of information can make a vital difference to the patient's treatment plan and care. A lengthy account will not be needed, but when you get a moment, you should jot down the following:

- Casualty's name and date of birth
- What happened and when
- Injuries
- Level of consciousness
- Pain location and intensity (you may want to grade it 1-10 with a score of 10 being the most intense pain they can imagine)
- Pulse (beats per minute)
- Treatment given
- Previous medical history of the casualty and details of any regular medication that is taken
- Allergies
- Anything else that you think might be relevant

This is a guide and there is always a need for common sense. Update your records as and when things change, as the rate of change in pain or pulse might be important.

Arriving at a hospital

As soon as the injured person is being looked after by medical professionals, you should contact their insurers if you have not already done so (you may consider informing the British consulate). Give them the information that you have recorded, as detailed above, and make sure you write down everything you are told. Keep a copy and make sure the insurer has your exact contact details, so that they can phone you back at a pre-arranged time. Stay with the casualty – you may end up doing all their nursing care and feeding them, and they will need someone to act as their advocate. Unless there really is a pressing need, I would not advise anyone to have surgery in a developing world country, or a blood transfusion unless the casualty is bleeding to death.

BEING AN EXPEDITION MEDIC

You might be a doctor, nurse, paramedic, operating department practitioner or an experienced first-aider and have been asked to be the medic on an expedition or wilderness trip of some kind. This can be a great challenge and a very fulfilling role, but you should be prepared. Below are some thoughts to reflect on:

- It is a significant responsibility and can be extremely hard work, as you are on call 24 hours a day, seven days a week. It requires a lot of preparation and commitment.
- You will need clinical skills, survival skills and inter-personal skills if you are going to do the job well. For more information on this, see my study on The Outdoor Experience website (see appendix).
- A medic who does not have the skills to look after themselves or reach a casualty in a wilderness environment can be more of a liability than a help.
- Most issues on a trip will be minor and may simply involve being a listening ear, but you should get trained so that you are confident in handling the situations listed in this chapter, just in case one happens. Books and courses are available.
- Your kit should be adequate but compact – as a guide, one or two 20-litre rucksack pockets should be large enough. Make sure everyone else has their travel survival kit and knows how to use it.
- Find out where the nearest medical facilities are and think about how you would evacuate someone in an emergency.
- Check you are insured to deliver care. Your professional body should be able to help on this.

11

RETURNING HOME

It can feel weird arriving home after your travels. You've had weeks, months or even years of an intense and varied life of adventure, excitement and meeting new people – then suddenly it all stops. You've been to all those places and experienced so much, and yet nothing may have changed at home.

Of course, it's great to be home, tanned and fit, with your rucksack and kit now proudly battered and worn. It's wonderful to see family and friends and tell them about your travels, and having your own bed back is very welcoming. You may feel elated, but it can also feel odd, almost as if you have been in a time warp. You may need time to acclimatise to being home, but you should remember that these are all natural reactions.

It may be that you have been exposed to a lot of poverty and you find it hard to adjust back to the affluence we have in the West. You may even start to go into haggling mode when you first go to the shops! It's like culture shock, but in reverse.

You may feel that your travelling experiences set you apart from those around you; yet you also know that you have to integrate back into society. Friends' attitudes may have changed, or they may have stayed the same but you see them differently, and they may see dramatic changes in you.

Finally, you may have come home to a debt from too much spending on your credit card. This can bring you down to earth with a real bump as you start to work to clear it. I remember getting home after a six-month adventure in America, getting off the bus in my home village and just standing there thinking, now what? Two days later I was cleaning toilets in a hospital in order to get some money. It was hard to adjust to the contrast.

Some people adapt immediately to their previous lifestyle and move on, others take a lot longer – we are all different.

If you do have trouble reconciling your experiences with being back home, how can you deal with this? Recognise your feelings and acknowledge that your recent adventures existed and are very real, even though it may all seem a lifetime ago. Reflect on them and enjoy the memories and what you have learned. Stay in touch with travelling friends, re-live shared experiences and organise reunions if appropriate. My friends and I still look back at our past adventures with real enjoyment years later, and the memories are as clear as ever. If you have been with a formal Gap organisation, they should organise a reunion or debrief.

Thereafter, how you approach life is up to you. You might apply what you have learned to whatever you do next, or you may opt to help others in the same way you were helped. Perhaps your travelling experiences will mean you decide on a completely new direction for your life. If you can get it together to go travelling, you should be able to put your experiences to positive use! Your Gap Year experience is a part of your life, and not something that should be seen as a separate entity.

It may be that you need to find a good friend who can listen to you if you are feeling down, or there may be an opportunity for you to help another traveller who needs someone sympathetic to talk to. If you continue to feel out of sorts, particularly if you have physical symptoms, you should consider getting a medical check-up as you may have picked up an infection whilst away.

It is important to occupy your time with something fulfilling. You may have studies to get on with, or work to go to, but get involved in some sort of organisation or activity that interests you. Value relaxation and allow yourself time to chill out and reflect on life. Hopefully, your time spent travelling will have equipped you with personal skills that you can transfer into your life as you move forward into more adventures, whether at home or abroad.

SO FINALLY.........

It's been great fun writing this book; it has been a journey in itself and provided many challenges. My hope is that by reading this book you will be able to head off on your trip better prepared and able to get the maximum enjoyment and benefit from it, whilst reducing unnecessary risk.

A spirit of adventure is so important in our lives – one of the great things about the increase in Gap Year initiatives and adventure travel is that it promotes the desire to push the limits of our daily lives. Travellers usually return more confident and self-reliant, with more autonomy and lateral thinking. This is to be encouraged! There is a real opportunity for personal development if you decide to break away from your comfort zone and grasp all that your trip has to offer.

After all, life is not a dress rehearsal. You've got one shot at it, so make it count.

APPENDIX

TRAVEL HEALTH-RELATED WEBSITES

There are many websites around these days related to all types of travel as well as travel health. The ones below are a selection of reliable sites; most have plenty of links to other sites and a web search will soon find what you are looking for if it is not listed in the pages below.

British Mountaineering Council	www.thebmc.co.uk
British Travel Health Association (BTHA)	www.btha.org
Department of Health	www.dh.gov.uk
Fit for Travel (excellent health advice)	www.fitfortravel.scot.nhs.uk
Foreign Office	www.fco.gov.uk
Passport Agency	www.ukpa.gov.uk
Stanfords (Maps)	www.stanfords.co.uk/
Sun Awareness	www.sunsmart.org.uk
The Outdoor Experience	www.outdoorex.co.uk
Wilderness Medical Society	www.wms.org
Year Out Group	www.yearoutgroup.org

INDEX

ABTA 15
accidents 102, 154, 155
accommodation 99-100
activities, choosing 125-130 *see also*
adventures, wild country
    aerial pursuits 128-130
    beach based 126
    bungee jumping 128-130
    canoeing 127-128
    scuba diving 127, 130
    white-water rafting 128
adventure tour operators 8-9, 132-133
adventures, wild country 130-133 *see
also* emergency survival skills; first-
aid, wilderness; sports, extreme
    organising 133
    research 131
    tour operators 8-9, 132-133
Africa 55-56, 132-133 *see also*
Botswana; Gambia; Kenya; Uganda;
Zambia; Zimbabwe
airports 97, 98
alcohol 116, 157-158
arrival 98-99
ATOL 15
Australia 103
    Kakadu National Park 158

baggage rules 97
bags 35, 37 *see also* rucksacks
batteries 31, 42 43, 91
behaviour 116, 119
'bivi bags' (breathable sleeping bag
covers) 30, 100 *see also* survival
bags, polythene
body language 120
Botswana, Chobe National Park 5
budgeting 14 *see also* money
management
bungee jumping 128-130

cameras 38-42 *see also* photography
    batteries for 42-43, 91

buying 40-41
carrying 41-42, 122
cases for 41-42, 122
compact 39-40, 42, 122
digital 39, 40
single lens reflex (SLR) 39, 40
camping 100
Canada 16, 30, 127
candles 31-32, 91, 135
canoeing 127-128
cashpoints 114
CDs 34, 97
charities 3-5, 13
clothing, personal 22-24, 27
    fleece tops 24
    gloves 27
    hats 27, 86, 146, 148
    and insect bites 23, 24, 60
    for jungles 145
    shirts 24, 145
    shorts 23
    skirts 23
    swimming costumes 27
    T-shirts 24
    trousers 22-23, 60, 145
    underwear 23
    washing 32
    waterproof 24-27, 134
        gaiters 31
        jackets 25-26
        overtrousers 25, 26-27
communication 109-111
compasses 33, 144
condoms 82, 117
contact lenses 32, 85, 91
contraception 81-82, 117
credit cards 15, 114, 173
cultures 80
    adjusting to 98-99, 119-124
    body language 120
    getting involved 120-121
    languages, learning basics of 120, 123
    medical care 121

respect for 119-120
taking pictures of local people 122-123
time-keeping 123-124
Customs 35, 90-91, 98

DEET 61
dehydration 69-70, 147, 148, 149, 169
deserts 146-147
    medical conditions 147-149
        heat exhaustion 147
        heat stroke 147, 148-149
Diabetes UK 77
Discman 34, 97
diseases 18, 44, 47 *see also* health
    carried by insects 58-67 *see also*
malaria
        insect repellents 60, 61, 62
        sleeping 61-62
    vaccine-preventable 49-58
        ACW135Y vaccine 53
        BCG vaccine 57
        cholera 58
        encephalitis 57-58
        hepatitis A 49-50
        hepatitis B 55-56, 117
        meningitis 52-53
        polio 51-52
        rabies 54-55
        tetanus 51
        tuberculosis (TB) 56-57
        typhoid 50-51
        yellow fever 18, 47-48, 53-54
diving, scuba 127, 130
documents 33, 92, 113
Dew, Josie 109
drugs 117-119

e-mails 111 *see also* internet
eating utensils 33, 145
emergency contact numbers 92, 113

emergency survival skills 134-135 *see
also* deserts; first-aid, wilderness; jungles;
        mountains
equipment 19 *see also* cameras; clothing;
footwear; sleeping equipment
        carrying your kit 35-38 *see also*
rucksacks
    jungle 145
    miscellaneous 30-34, 91
Everest, Mount 135
expedition companies 6-7

finance 12-14, 126, 173-174 *see also*
money
first-aid, wilderness 150-172 *see also*
health; medic, expedition, acting as
    bites 151
    bleeding 153, 159-160, 165-166
    blisters 151
    burns 151-152
    colds 151
    consciousness, level of 161
    convulsions 161-162
    cuts 151
    dislocations 163, 165
    ear infections 151
    fainting 152
    fits 161-162
    flu 151
    fractures 163-165, 169
    head injuries 160-162
    hospital, arriving at 171-172
    medical conditions, more serious 153-172
        airway 153, 156-158
        assessment (approach) 153, 154-156
        breathing 153, 156-158
        circulation 153, 159-160
        disability 154, 160-162
        evacuation 154, 161, 166-168
        exposure 154, 163
        survey, primary 153, 154-160
        survey, secondary 154, 160-168

minor ailments 151-152
moving a casualty 166-167, 168
neck injuries 160, 162
nursing issues 168-171
  confidentiality and dignity 168-
169
  fluid and food intake 169-170
  record keeping 170-171
  toilet needs 169-170
rashes 151
snake bites 166
spinal injuries 160, 162, 163
sprains 163, 164, 165
stings 151 *see also* insect bites
wounds, open 165
first-aid (travel survival) kits 31-32,
86-92, 133
  antibiotics 89-90
  bandages/dressings 88-89, 159,
166
  gloves, surgical 89, 159, 165, 170
  key points 87
  medical items 87-91
  medication 89-91 *see also*
medication
  non-medical items 91-92
  plasters 86, 88
  sterile supplies kits 91
  wipes, cleaning 68, 88
food 72-76, 100-101
  in emergency situations 135
  personal experience 75-76
  reducing risk of Delhi belly 73-74
  see also health: diarrhoea, travellers'
footwear 19-22, 109, 145
  boots, walking 20-21, 145
  sandals 22
  socks 21-22, 60
  trainers 19-20, 21, 109
Foreign Office 11, 102
friendships, maintaining 115-116,
121, 174

Gambia 65-66
gap year companies 3-4
glasses 85
Gore-Tex 21, 25, 30, 100
Grieve, Sandra 46-48, 79-82
guide books 11, 46, 99, 131

Handley, Bob 69
health 44-92 *see also* deserts: medical
conditions; diseases; first-aid *entries*;
food;   insect bites; malaria; medication;
mountains: medical conditions; water
  advice 45-48
  bowel problems 68-69
  deep vein thrombosis (DVT) 78-79, 81
  diarrhoea, travellers' 68, 69, 70, 82,
169
    reducing risk of 73-74
    treating 76, 90
  ear infections 90, 151
  eye care 33, 84-85 *see also* sunglasses
  hygiene 68-69, 101
  jungle problems 145
  medical conditions, pre-existing 48,
77-78
  medication 35, 77, 89-91
  preparation 44-45
  on returning home 174
  sexually transmitted infections (STIs)
55, 82, 117
  skin care 85-86, 90
  stomach problems 68-69, 70, 73-74
  teeth 83-84, 90
  urinary tract infection 90
  vaccinations 44, 45, 46, 48-49
  women's 79-82
    contraception 81-82, 117
    fluid retention 81
    hygiene, personal 80
    menstruation 80-81
    pregnancy 17, 80, 82
Himalayas 12, 34, 136 *see also* Everest,
Mount; Nepal

hitch-hiking 107-108
hygiene, personal 68-69, 80, 101
hypothermia 25, 37, 134, 136-138, 141, 154, 163

independent travel, planning 9-11
India 32, 74, 75-76, 99, 103, 127, 132-133 *see also* Kashmir
   Delhi 104, 107
   Northern 10
insect bites 23, 24, 44, 53, 57, 58, 151 *see also* malaria; mosquito bites/nets
insect repellents 60, 61, 62
insects, diseases carried by *see* diseases: carried by insects
insurance 15-17
   adventure sports 16
   dental cover 84
   details 92, 113
   emergencies 17
   medical treatment, contacting company 167, 171
   pregnancy 17
internet 99, 109, 110, 111, 114, 131

job seeking 12, 13 *see also* working
jungles 143-146
   equipment 145
   navigation 143, 144
   overnight stops 144-145
   rivers 144
   water in 143

Kashmir 74
   Dal Lake 14
Kenya
   Lake Turkana 146
   Mount Kenya 20, 132, 136
knives, Swiss Army 30-31, 87, 134, 165

Lane, Bronco 135, 143-146, 168

languages, learning basics of 120, 123
'Leatherman' gadgets 31
letters 109-110, 111
Lonely Planet guides 11, 46, 100

malaria 59-60 *see also* diseases: carried by insects; mosquito bites/nets
   avoiding being bitten 60, 61, 65
   awareness of the danger 60
   diagnosing 67
   key points 65
   medication, preventive 32, 62-65
      chloroquine (Avloclor or Nivaquine) 63-64
      doxycycline 65, 86, 117
      mefloquine (Lariam) 64, 82
      proguanil (Paludrine) 63-64
      proguanil with atovaquone (Malarone) 63, 64-65
   personal experience 65-67
   treating 67
maps 33, 131, 136, 144
matches 32, 91, 135
Matthews, Dr Hugh 8-9, 133
medic, expedition, acting as 172
medical conditions, pre-existing 48, 77-78
medication 35, 77, 89-91 *see also* malaria: medication, preventive
money 33 *see also* finance
   safety and security 112-113
money management 113-114 *see also* budgeting
Mont Blanc, Tour du 10-11
mosquito bites 53, 57, 59 *see also* insect bites; malaria
mosquito nets 61
mountains 136, 141-142
   medical conditions 136-143
      acute mountain sickness (AMS) 138, 139-140
      frostbite 142-143
      frostnip 142

high-altitude cerebral oedema
(HACE) 138, 141
   high-altitude pulmonary oedema
(HAPE) 138, 140
   high-altitude sickness 138-139
   hypothermia 25, 37, 134, 136-
138, 141, 154, 163
  sleeping in 141
MP3 players 34
mugs 33
music 119

National Geographic magazine 43
Nepal 10, 29, 34, 132-133 *see also*
Everest, Mount; Himalayas
New Zealand 30, 129-130
Norwegian Arctic 88, 136
nylon cord 31, 91, 134

organisers, nylon 33

paperwork 33, 92, 113
parents 12
passports 18
penknives 30-31, 87, 134, 165
people, getting on with 115-116
people, local *see* cultures
Peru 123-124
phones, mobile 110, 111
photography 38-43 *see also* cameras
  batteries 42-43, 91
  film 39-40, 42
  lenses 39, 40, 123
  pictures, developing 43
  pictures, taking 43, 122-123
planning 2-18
  choice, making 11
  finance 12-14, 126
  health 44-45
  independent travel 9-11
  insurance *see* insurance
  organised and semi-organised
adventures 2-9

parents 12
tickets 14-15
visas 17-18
when and where to go 11-12
work permits 17-18
Post Restante system 111
pregnancy 17, 80, 82

radios, short-wave 34
rafting, white-water 128
relationships, maintaining 115-116, 121,
174
returning home 173-175
Rough Guide books 11, 46, 100
Royal Army Medical Corps, Combat
Medical Technicians 133
rucksacks 19, 35-37, 106
  waterproof liners 35, 37-38, 106

safety 11, 108, 112-113, 118, 154
  emergency survival skills 134-135 *see
also* deserts; first-aid, wilderness; jungles;
mountains
  water 126, 128
  women's 80, 82
safety pins 91
Saudi Arabia 53
security *see* safety
sewing kit 91
sex 55, 82, 116-117
Shrewsbury NHS Trust ITU 52, 53
skin care 85-86, 90, 91
sky diving 130
sleeping equipment 28-30 *see also*
survival bags, polythene
  and insect bites 61-62
  sleeping bag covers, breathable ('bivi
bags') 30, 100
  sleeping bag liners, silk 29
  sleeping bags 28-29
  sleeping mats 29-30
  thermarests 30
snake bites 166

The Gap Year Handbook.

snow blindness 33, 85
sports, extreme 128-130
  insurance for 16
Stanfords 33, 176
Stokes, Brummie 135
stoves 34
summer camps in the USA 7-8, 38, 54, 127
sunburn and protection 85-86, 91, 146
sunglasses 32-33, 84, 85, 146
survival bags, polythene 134, 138 *see also* 'bivi bags'
survival skills, emergency 134-135 *see also* deserts; first-aid, wilderness; jungles; mountains

tarps, nylon ('basha sheets') 30, 100
telephones 110-111
tents 34
Thailand 74, 100, 113, 126, 130
tickets 14-15
time, managing 125-126 *see also* activities, choosing
toilet paper 34, 81
torches 31, 165
tour operators, adventure 8-9, 132-133
transport 101-109
  aircraft 102
  animals 109
  bikes 108-109
  boats 106
  buses 102-104
  cars 105
  coaches 102-104, 107
  four-wheel drive vehicles (4WD) 105-106
  hitch-hiking 107-108
  local 104
  motorbikes 106
  risk, reducing 102
  taxis 104

trains 107
trucks 105
travel agents 14-15
travel clinics 46

Uganda 60, 123, 127
USA 103-104, 107, 117, 136
  Longs Peak, Denver 139
  San Francisco 151
  summer camps 7-8, 38, 54, 127
  Washington State 131, 136

vaccinations 44, 45, 46, 48-49 *see also* diseases: vaccine-preventable
visas 17-18

walking 109 *see also* footwear
washkits 32
water 69-72
  boiling 71
  bottled 70
  chemical treatment 71-72, 91
  dehydration 69-70, 147, 148, 149, 169
  in deserts 146-147, 148
  in emergency situations 135
  filtration 71
  in the jungle 143
  key points 72
water accidents 155
water bottles 33, 68, 72
water sports 126-128
women and culture/clothing 80 *see also* health, women's
work permits 17-18
working 125 *see also* job seeking
World Health Organisation (WHO) 54, 57

Zambia 4-5
Zimbabwe 6-7